S E R I E S

A life-changing encounter
with God's Word from the books of

EZRA &

NEHEMIAH

NAVPRESS

*A NavPress resource published in alliance
with Tyndale House Publishers, Inc.*

NAVPRESS⊘

NavPress is the publishing ministry of The Navigators, an international Christian organization and leader in personal spiritual development. NavPress is committed to helping people grow spiritually and enjoy lives of meaning and hope through personal and group resources that are biblically rooted, culturally relevant, and highly practical.

For more information, visit www.NavPress.com.

Ezra and Nehemiah

Copyright © 2011 by The Navigators. All rights reserved.

A NavPress resource published in alliance with Tyndale House Publishers, Inc.

NAVPRESS and the NAVPRESS logo are registered trademarks of NavPress, The Navigators, Colorado Springs, CO. Absence of ® in connection with marks of NavPress or other parties does not indicate an absence of registration of those marks. *TYNDALE* is a registered trademark of Tyndale House Publishers, Inc.

All Scripture quotations, unless otherwise indicated, are taken from the Holy Bible, *New International Version*,® *NIV*.® Copyright © 1973, 1978, 1984, 2011 by Biblica, Inc.® Used by permission. All rights reserved worldwide. Scripture quotations marked NASB are taken from the New American Standard Bible,® copyright © 1960, 1962, 1963, 1968, 1971, 1972, 1973, 1975, 1977, 1995 by The Lockman Foundation. Used by permission. Scripture quotations marked ESV are taken from *The Holy Bible*, English Standard Version® (ESV®), copyright © 2001 by Crossway, a publishing ministry of Good News Publishers. Used by permission. All rights reserved.

ISBN 978-1-61521-728-1

Printed in the United States of America

21 20 19 18 17 16
10   9   8   7   6

CONTENTS

HOW TO USE THIS GUIDE

Although the LIFECHANGE guides vary with the individual books they explore, they share some common goals:

1. To provide you with a firm foundation of understanding, plus a thirst to return to the book throughout your life

2. To give you study patterns and skills that help you explore every part of the Bible

3. To offer you historical background, word definitions, and explanation notes to aid your study

4. To help you grasp the message of the book as a whole

5. To teach you how to let God's Word transform you into Christ's image

As You Begin

This guide includes eight lessons, which will take you chapter by chapter through all of Ezra and Nehemiah. Each lesson is designed to take from one to two hours of preparation to complete on your own. To benefit most from this time, here's a good way to begin your work on each lesson:

1. Pray for God's help to keep you mentally alert and spiritually sensitive.

2. Read attentively through the entire passage mentioned in the lesson's title. (You may want to read the passage from two or more Bible versions—perhaps at least once from a more literal translation such as the New International Version, English Standard Version, New American Standard Bible, or New King James Version, and perhaps once more in a paraphrase such as *The Message* or the New Living Translation.) Do your reading in an environment that's as free as possible from distractions. Allow your mind and heart to meditate on the words you encounter—words that are God's personal gift to you and to all His people.

After reading the passage, you're ready to dive into the numbered questions in this guide, which make up the main portion of each lesson. Each of these questions is followed by blank space for writing your answers. This act of writing your answers helps clarify your thinking and stimulates your mental engagement with the passage as well as your later recall. Use extra paper or a notebook if the space for recording your answers seems too cramped. Continue through the questions in numbered order. If any question seems too difficult or unclear, just skip it and go on to the next.

Most of these questions will direct you back to Ezra or Nehemiah to look again at a certain portion of the assigned passage for that lesson. At this point, be sure to use a more literal Bible translation rather than a paraphrase.

As you look closer at the passage, it's helpful to approach it in this progression:

Observe. What does the passage actually *say*? Ask God to help you see it clearly. Notice everything that's there.

Interpret. What does the passage *mean*? Ask God to help you understand. And remember that any passage's meaning is fundamentally determined by its *context*. Stay alert to all you'll see about the setting and background of Ezra and Nehemiah, and keep thinking of these books as a whole while you proceed through them chapter by chapter. You'll be progressively building up your insights and familiarity with what they're all about.

Apply. Keep asking yourself, *How does this truth affect my life?* Pray for God's help as you examine yourself in light of that truth, and in light of His purpose for each passage.

Try to consciously follow all three of these approaches as you shape your written answer to each question in the lesson.

The Extras

In addition to the regular numbered questions you see in this guide, each lesson also offers several "optional" questions or suggestions that appear in the margins. All of these will appear under one of three headings:

Optional Application. Try as many of these questions as you can without overcommitting yourself, considering them with prayerful sensitivity to the Lord's guidance.

For Thought and Discussion. Many of these questions address various ethical issues and other biblical principles that lead to a wide range of implications. They tend to be particularly suited for group discussions.

For Further Study. These often include cross-references to other parts of the Bible that shed light on a topic in the lesson, plus questions that delve deeper into the passage.

(For additional help for more effective Bible study, refer to the "Study Aids" section beginning on page 129.)

Changing Your Life

Don't let your study become an exercise in knowledge alone. Treat the passage as God's Word, and stay in dialogue with Him as you study. Pray, "Lord, what do You want me to notice here?" "Father, why is this true?" "Lord, how does my life measure up to this?"

Let biblical truth sink into your inner convictions so you'll increasingly be able to act on this truth as a natural way of living.

At times you may want to consider memorizing a certain verse or passage you come across in your study, one that particularly challenges or encourages you. To help with that, write down the words on a card to keep with you, and set aside a few minutes each day to think about the passage. Recite it to yourself repeatedly, always thinking about its meaning. Return to it as often as you can, for a brief review. You'll soon find the words coming to mind spontaneously, and they'll begin to affect your motives and actions.

For Group Study

Exploring Scripture together in a group is especially valuable for the encouragement, support, and accountability it provides as you seek to apply God's Word to your life. Together you can listen jointly for God's guidance, pray for each other, help one another resist temptation, and share the spiritual principles you're learning to put into practice. Together you affirm that growing in faith, hope, and love is important and that you need each other in the process.

A group of four to ten people allows for the closest understanding of each other and the richest discussions in Bible study, but you can adapt this guide for other-sized groups. It will suit a wide range of group types, such as home Bible studies, growth groups, youth groups, and church classes. Both new and mature Christians will benefit from the guide, regardless of their previous experience in Bible study.

Aim for a positive atmosphere of acceptance, honesty, and openness. In your first meeting, explore candidly everyone's expectations and goals for your time together.

A typical schedule for group study is to take one lesson per week, but feel free to split lessons if you want to discuss them more thoroughly. Or omit some questions in a lesson if your preparation or discussion time is limited. (You can always return to this guide later for further study on your own.)

When you come together, you probably won't have time to discuss all the questions in the lesson, so it's helpful to choose ahead of time the ones you want to make sure to cover thoroughly. This is one of the main responsibilities that a group leader typically assumes.

Each lesson in this guide ends with a section called "For the Group." It gives advice for that particular lesson on how to focus the discussion, how to apply the lesson to daily life, and so on. Reading each lesson's "For the Group" section ahead of time can help the leader be more effective in guiding the group.

You'll get the greatest benefit from your time together if each group member also prepares ahead of time by writing out his or her answers to each question in the lesson. The private reflection and prayer that this preparation can stimulate will be especially important in helping everyone discern how God wants you to apply each lesson to your daily life.

There are many ways to structure the group meeting, and in fact you may want to vary your routine occasionally to help keep things fresh.

Here are some of the elements you can consider including as you come together for each lesson:

Pray together. It's good to pause for prayer as you begin your time together. When you begin with prayer, it's worthwhile and honoring to God to ask especially for His Holy Spirit's guidance of your time together. If you write down each other's prayer requests, you are more likely to remember to pray for them during the week, ask about them at the next meeting, and notice answered prayers. You might want to get a notebook for prayer requests and discussion notes.

Worship. Some groups like to sing together and worship God with prayers of praise.

Review. You may want to take time to discuss what difference the previous week's lesson has made in your life as well as recall the major emphasis you discovered in the passage for that week.

Read the passage aloud. Once you're ready to focus attention together on the assigned Scripture passage in the week's lesson, read it aloud. (One person could do this, or the reading could be shared.)

Open up for lingering questions. Allow time for the group members to mention anything in the passage that they may have particular questions about.

Summarize the passage. Have one or two people offer a summary of what the passage tells about.

Discuss. This will be the heart of your time together and will likely take the biggest portion of your time. Focus on the questions you see as the most important and most helpful. Allow and encourage everyone to be part of the discussion for each question. You may want to take written notes as the discussion proceeds. Ask follow-up questions to sharpen your attention and deepen your understanding of what you discuss. You may want to give special attention to the questions in the margin under the heading "For Thought and Discussion."

Encourage further personal study. You can find more opportunities for exploring the lesson's themes and issues under the marginal heading "For Further Study" throughout the lesson. You can also pursue some of these together, during your group time.

Focus on application. Look especially at the "Optional Application" sections found in the margins. Keep encouraging one another in the continual work of adjusting your lives to the truths God gives in Scripture.

Summarize your discoveries. You may want to read aloud through the passage one last time together, using the opportunity to solidify your understanding and appreciation of it and to clarify how the Lord is speaking to you through it.

Look ahead. Glance together at the headings and questions in the next lesson to see what's coming next.

Give thanks to God. It's good to end your time together by pausing to express gratitude to God for His Word and for the work of His Spirit in your minds and hearts during your time together.

Keep these worthy guidelines in mind throughout your time together:

Let us consider how we may spur one another on toward love and good deeds.

(HEBREWS 10:24)

Carry each other's burdens, and in this way you will fulfill the law of Christ.

(GALATIANS 6:2)

Accept one another, then, just as Christ accepted you, in order to bring praise to God.

(ROMANS 15:7)

9

TIMELINE

A Chronological Background of Ezra and Nehemiah

In the following chart, some of the approximate dates listed have varying degrees of scholarly support or disagreement.[1]

Approximate Date	Major International Events	Events in Palestine
722 BC		Israel (Northern Kingdom) falls to Assyrian Empire (2 Kings 17:6-18)
605	Assyrian Empire replaced by Babylonian Empire, with Nebuchadnezzar as king (Daniel 1–2)	
586		Judah (Southern Kingdom) falls to Babylonian Empire; Jerusalem destroyed (2 Kings 25:1-21; 2 Chronicles 36:13-21)
562	Babylon's King Nebuchadnezzar dies	
550	Belshazzar begins reign as Babylon's last king (Daniel 7:1)	
539	Babylon Empire taken over by the Medians and Persians, under Cyrus and Darius (Daniel 5:30-31; 11:1)	
538		Cyrus issues proclamation allowing Jewish exiles to return to Judea (2 Chronicles 36:22-23; Ezra 1:1-4)
537		Sheshbazzar leads group of Jewish exiles in return from Babylon to Judea (Ezra 1:11); altar is rebuilt at site of destroyed temple (Ezra 3:1-3)
536		Rebuilding of temple begins in Jerusalem (Ezra 3:8)
536–530		Adversaries oppose rebuilding of temple (Ezra 4:1-5)

Approximate Date	Major International Events	Events in Palestine
530–520 BC		Temple rebuilding ceases (Ezra 4:24)
529	Cyrus dies	
523	Persians conquer Egypt; Darius attains full power over Persian Empire (Daniel 6; 9:1)	
520s		More Jewish exiles, including Zerubbabel and Joshua, return to Judea
520		Rebuilding of temple resumes (Ezra 5:1-2; Haggai 1:12-15)
516		Temple construction completed (Ezra 6:13-18)
490	Greeks win battle at Marathon, halting westward expansion of Persian Empire	
486	Darius succeeded by Xerxes (Ahasuerus in Ezra 4:6; see also the book of Esther)	
480	Greeks again defeat Persians, this time at Salamis	
465	Xerxes (Ahasuerus) succeeded by Artaxerxes I as king of the Persian Empire	
458		Ezra returns from Babylon to Jerusalem and ministers there (Ezra 7–10)
445		Nehemiah journeys to Jerusalem and leads restoration of city walls (Nehemiah 1–7); Ezra leads in spiritual revival (Nehemiah 8–10)
445–433		Nehemiah serves as governor in Judah (Nehemiah 5:14)
433–432		Nehemiah travels to Susa (Persian capital), then returns to Jerusalem (Nehemiah 13:6-7)
424	Artaxerxes I dies	
335–323	Alexander the Great rises to power, then conquers Persian Empire	

1. This timeline is adapted from charts and data in the *ESV Study Bible* (Wheaton, IL: Crossway, 2008) in commentary on the books of Ezra, Nehemiah, and Daniel and from data in F. Charles Fensham, *The Books of Ezra and Nehemiah* (Grand Rapids, MI: Eerdmans, 1982), 9–16.

THE BOOK OF EZRA

A People Restored, a Temple Rebuilt

The book of Ezra brings us welcome good news after the tragic destruction of Jerusalem and the exile into captivity of the Jews, as recorded in the final pages of 2 Kings and 2 Chronicles. The story in Ezra is told not as a mere historical record but as a testimony to God's sovereignty, love, and wisdom. His presence is strongly felt in this account. "The Book of Ezra reveals the providential intervention of the God of heaven on behalf of his people."[1]

An Inevitable Story

The story we find in Ezra is, in a sense, inevitable. God Himself had promised a restoration for His people, and the faithful ones among them had clung to this hope. So the book of Ezra sprang forth not as a detached account of events but as a worshipful portrait of God's ever-continuing faithfulness.

"The object of Ezra was not to give a history of the resettlement in Judah and Jerusalem. . . . It is evident that the object and plan . . . must have been to collect only such facts and documents as might show the manner in which the Lord God, after the lapse of the seventy years of exile, fulfilled His promise announced by the prophets—by the deliverance of His people from Babylon, the building of the temple at Jerusalem, and the restoration of the temple worship according to the law—and preserved the reassembled community from fresh relapses into heathen customs and idolatrous worship by the dissolution of the marriages with Gentile women."[2]

In reading this record of God's faithfulness, we're pointed to truths that are emphasized throughout Scripture, especially the importance of right worship and the need to be faithful and patiently enduring in the face of difficulty.

"It is clear that these chapters were not intended to provide a full account of postexilic Jewish history. Rather, the author recorded only certain instances which he regarded as important for understanding Jewish religious development in this period. Of primary importance for his purpose are those selected facts which emphasize the continual Samaritan opposition to the reconstruction of Jewish religious life and the reorganization of the religious community by the building of an altar and the eventual reconstruction of the temple."[3]

The Background of Disrupted Worship

In its historical setting, the book of Ezra brings in rays of light for God's people after decades of darkness in their Promised Land.

"When Nebuchadnezzar finally demolished Jerusalem in 586 BC . . . a large portion of the most important Jews, especially artisans and craftsmen, were carried to Babylon in exile. With the temple in ruins, the Jews left behind had no place to worship the Lord properly. Although an altar was erected on the site of the demolished temple, the official cult was for all practical purposes terminated. . . . The Jews in Palestine were poor and thus not able to restore the damage done to their country."[4]

This darkness was centered especially on the temple's destruction and all that this meant for God's people.

"One of the most important functions of the temple was to provide opportunity to atone for sins by sacrifice (later aptly described in Hebrews 9). On the Day of Atonement the high priest was required to enter the Holy of Holies to atone for his own sins and for those of his people. Throughout pre-exilic times, the Israelites were assured by this religious practice that their sins were forgiven by the Lord. . . . With the destruction of the temple, this privilege had been taken away. This must be regarded as one of the major catastrophes which had overtaken the Jews. Their whole religious life was disorganized by it. It is thus not surprising that the first act after the restoration was to build an altar and to begin reconstruction of the temple. Now for the first time since the Exile the Jews were able to atone properly for their sins. The rebuilding of the temple was not simply an act of restoration of a venerable old building, but was of the highest religious significance."[5]

The World Scene

The events God orchestrated to bring about His people's restoration to the Promised Land included a transition of empires, from Babylon to Persia.

Babylon had been slipping into decline in the sixth century BC. "The scene was perfectly set for a takeover by a foreign country. To the northeast, in the mountains of Iran, the young Persian king Cyrus succeeded in gaining control over the Indo-Arian Medes. The Persians and the Medes became a formidable combination. Cyrus had great aspirations. . . . Step by step he built up an empire and soon became strong enough to tackle the Babylonian empire. . . . Babylon and the Babylonian empire with it fell into the hands of Cyrus without any significant resistance in 539 BC."[6]

For the Jews who had been taken captive into Babylonia, this was a welcome change indeed.

"Cyrus was an enlightened and tolerant king. After his seizure of Babylon he released an edict in which he promised displaced peoples a return to their countries and the right to rebuild the sanctuaries of their gods. This is quite an opposite policy to that followed by the Babylonians. At the same time it was a realistic policy that would create the maximum amount of contentment among the peoples under the jurisdiction of the Persians. This created an excellent occasion for the exiled Jews in Babylon to return to Judah and to rebuild the temple of the Lord in Jerusalem."[7]

This open opportunity was warmly taken up by the Jews whose hearts God had inspired, as we see in the events unfolding in the book of Ezra.

Authorship of This Book

Various theories have been put forward by scholars associating the authorship of the book of Ezra in some way with that of 1 and 2 Chronicles and Nehemiah. The books of Ezra and Nehemiah were combined in many ancient Hebrew manuscripts. "Given his literary skills (7:6), Ezra may well have been the compiler of the books of Ezra and Nehemiah, as is held by Jewish tradition."[8]

The book of Ezra includes first-person extracts from his memoirs (see 7:27-28; 8:1-34; 9) as well as sections where Ezra is referred to in third person (see 7:1-26; 10; Nehemiah 8). "Linguistic analysis has shown that the first-person and third-person extracts resemble each other, making it likely that the same author wrote both."[9]

The book also includes a number of lists and several official documents and letters.

1. Edwin M. Yamauchi, *Ezra-Nehemiah*, in vol. 4 of *The Expositor's Bible Commentary*, ed. Frank E. Gabelein (Grand Rapids, MI: Zondervan, 1990), 590.
2. C. F. Keil, *Ezra, Nehemiah, Esther*, vol. 4, in C. F. Keil and F. Delitzsch, *Commentary on the Old Testament* (Peabody, MA: Hendrickson, n.d.; original edition published by T. & T. Clark, Edinburgh, U.K., 1866–1891), 4–5.
3. F. Charles Fensham, *The Books of Ezra and Nehemiah* (Grand Rapids, MI: Eerdmans, 1982), 5–6.
4. Fensham, 9.
5. Fensham, 16–17.
6. Fensham, 10.
7. Fensham, 10–11.
8. *New Geneva Study Bible* (Nashville: Thomas Nelson, 1995), introduction to Ezra, "Author."
9. *NIV Study Bible* (Grand Rapids, MI: Zondervan, 1985), introduction to Ezra, "Literary Form and Authorship."

EZRA 1–3

A New Beginning

*With praise and thanksgiving they sang to the
Lord: "He is good; his love toward Israel endures
forever." And all the people gave a great shout
of praise to the Lord, because the foundation of
the house of the Lord was laid.*

EZRA 3:11

1. For getting the most from Ezra, one of the best
   guidelines is found in 2 Timothy 3:16-17, words
   Paul wrote with the Old Testament first in view.
   He said that *all* Scripture is of great benefit to
   (a) teach us, (b) rebuke us, (c) correct us, and
   (d) train us in righteousness. Paul added that
   these Scriptures completely equip the person
   of God "for every good work." As you think
   seriously about those guidelines, in which of
   these areas do you especially want to experience
   the usefulness of Ezra? Express your desire in
   a written prayer to God.

   _____

   _____

   _____

   _____

   _____

   _____

Optional Application: We read that after Jesus' resurrection, when He was explaining Old Testament passages to His disciples, He "opened their minds so they could understand the Scriptures" (Luke 24:45). Ask God to do that kind of work in *your* mind as you study Ezra so you're released and free to learn everything here He wants you to learn and so you can become as bold and worshipful and faithful as those early disciples of Jesus were. Express this desire to Him in prayer.

_____

_____

2. In Jeremiah 23:29, God says that His Word is like fire and like a hammer. He can use the Scriptures to burn away unclean thoughts and desires in our hearts. He can also use Scripture, with hammer-like hardness, to crush and crumble our spiritual hardness. From your study of Ezra, how do you most want to see the "fire and hammer" power of God's Word at work in your own life? Again, express this longing in a written prayer to God.

_____

_____

_____

_____

_____

_____

_____

3. Think about these words of Paul to his younger helper Timothy: "Do your best to present yourself to God as one approved, a worker who does not need to be ashamed and who correctly handles the word of truth" (2 Timothy 2:15). As you study God's word of truth in Ezra, He calls you to be a "worker." It takes *work*—concentration and perseverance—to fully appropriate God's blessings for us in this book. Express here your commitment before God to work diligently in this study of Ezra.

_____

_____

_____

_____

18

4. In one sitting, read through all of this short book of Ezra at least once. What stands out to you most about this book?

_____

_____

_____

_____

For Further Study: For helpful background to the events in the book of Ezra, look especially at 2 Kings 25 and 2 Chronicles 36. How would you summarize these background events?

5. How would you outline the major parts of the book of Ezra?

_____

_____

_____

_____

_____

6. Glance again through the pages of Ezra, looking for a theme or thought that recurs in the following verses: 1:2-3,5; 4:3; 5:11; 6:14; 9:9. What is that theme? Why is it important to God, and why is it important for all of God's people in all ages?

_____

_____

_____

_____

Help in High Places

Read through all of Ezra 1 again.

7. In the opening verse of the book of Ezra, what important purpose is given for God's actions?

_____

_____

For Further Study: In Daniel 9, look at how Daniel responded to the same prophecies of Jeremiah referred to in Ezra 1 and 2 Chronicles 36:21-22. To what extent are Daniel's prayers being answered in the book of Ezra?

In the first year of Cyrus (1:1). The year is thought to be 538 BC.

In order to fulfill the word of the LORD spoken by Jeremiah (1:1). "The whole book of Ezra is the story of God's work to fulfill his promises by bringing his people back from exile and establishing them once again in their land."[1] See also the repetition for emphasis in 2 Chronicles 36:21-22.

8. Summarize what Jeremiah prophesied in these passages, especially as they relate to the events unfolding in the book of Ezra:

   a. Jeremiah 25:11-14

   _____

   _____

   b. Jeremiah 29:10

   _____

   _____

   c. Jeremiah 32:36-38

   _____

   _____

   d. Jeremiah 33:7-13

   _____

   _____

This is what Cyrus king of Persia says (1:2). "The decree of Cyrus, acknowledging Jehovah, is in harmony with Cyrus's favorable references to Babylonian deities in contemporary records. This is a public decree, written in terms that would appeal to the Jews."[2]

9. Examine Cyrus's proclamation in 1:2-4. What exactly did he say he intended to accomplish? What reasons did he state for wanting to accomplish this? What does this proclamation indicate about Cyrus's attitude and beliefs regarding the Lord God?

_____

_____

_____

_____

For Further Study: What do you learn about Cyrus from Isaiah's prophecies about him two centuries earlier? (See especially Isaiah 44:28 and 45:1-7; see also 41:2-4, 25; 46:11; 48:14-15.) How might these ancient prophecies have influenced the thinking of Ezra about Cyrus?

"Three themes of Ezra and Nehemiah can be found in the decree of Cyrus (1:2-4). First, rebuilding the temple in Jerusalem is God's objective in the history of redemption at this point; second, the people of God as a whole, and not merely the great leaders, are vital for accomplishing this purpose. Third, the written word is a powerful tool used by God to accomplish His objective."[3]

For Thought and Discussion: Considering that God worked through King Cyrus of Persia on behalf of His purposes and His people, how do you think He might be working through powerful political leaders today?

10. What is important to note about the response to Cyrus's proclamation as recorded in 1:5-11?

_____

_____

_____

_____

11. Reading between the lines, what can you discern about the economic condition of the Jewish exiles at this point?

_____

_____

For Thought and Discussion: What kinds of emotions can you imagine were experienced by the returning exiles as they made their way to the land God had promised to their people?

A Happy List

Read through all of Ezra 2 again.

12. Why do you think the list in Ezra 2 of the returning exiles is included in God's Word? What purposes can you suggest, both for the original audience of the book of Ezra as well as for God's people in all ages?

_____

_____

_____

_____

_____

These are the people of the province who came up from the captivity of the exiles (2:1). The long list of returning exiles in Ezra 2 is repeated almost exactly in Nehemiah 7. "It is not clear . . . in Ezra 2 and Nehemiah 7 . . . whether personal names or family names are used. . . . The great majority of names in Ezra-Nehemiah are Hebrew names formed according to certain old principles. Some of the names had a longer history of usage . . . others a shorter time. . . . Other names occur for the first time in Ezra-Nehemiah."[4]

Zerubbabel (2:2). A descendant of David's royal line, and the appointed governor of the Jews. Zerubbabel is mentioned also in Ezra 3:2, 3:8, 4:1-3, and 5:2 as well as in Nehemiah 7:7, 12:1, and 12:47. He also plays a prominent role in the books of Haggai and Zechariah, the prophets who were active during the time when the temple in Jerusalem was rebuilt. "Zerubbabel was the last of the Davidic line to be entrusted with political authority by the occupying powers."[5]

13. Turn to the New Testament and find where Zerubbabel is listed in the genealogies of Jesus Christ given in Matthew 1:1-17 and Luke 3:23-28. In what verses is Zerubbabel named . . .

in Matthew 1?

_____

_____

in Luke 3?

_____

_____

Joshua (2:2). This high priest's name means "Yahweh saves"; the Greek form is Jesus. Joshua is also mentioned together with Zerubbabel in Ezra 3:2, 3:8, 4:1-3, and 5:2 and in Nehemiah 7:7 and 12:1. He is also prominent in Haggai and Zechariah.

"The Lord . . . raised up for His people, when delivered from Babylon, men like Zerubbabel their governor, Joshua [Jeshua] the high priest, and Ezra the scribe, who, supported by the prophets Haggai and Zechariah, undertook the work to which they were called, with hearty resolution, and carried it out with a powerful hand."[6]

14. Zerubbabel and Joshua are the first of a group of men named in 2:2 at the head of the list of returnees; these were the leaders of the group. How many leaders were there?

_____

_____

For Further Study: What prophecy is made about Zerubbabel in Haggai 2:20-23, and how might this relate both to the events Zerubbabel is a part of in the book of Ezra and to the Davidic line that culminates in Christ Jesus?

For Further Study: Review the prophetic vision in Zechariah 4 that includes Zerubbabel. What role does it envision for Zerubbabel? Also, how does this vision illustrate the ministry of God's Holy Spirit, and in what way does this relate to the events described in the book of Ezra?

For Further Study:
Review the prophetic vision about Joshua in Zechariah 3:1-10. How does this vision illustrate God's grace, and how does this grace relate to the events described in the book of Ezra?

For Further Study:
Look at the prophecy given about Joshua in Zechariah 6:9-15. How might this relate to the events Joshua is a part of in the book of Ezra and also to the future role of Christ Jesus?

Nehemiah . . . Mordecai (2:2). These are not the same men who are mentioned in the books of Nehemiah and Esther and who lived at a later time.

"Zerubbabel himself kept well clear of any politically questionable involvement; indeed, the biblical material gives the impression that he did not seek to advance himself but rather waited for others to motivate him to act. It is thus appropriate that nothing of his personal history is known after his significant role in rebuilding the second temple."[7]

15. Why do you think the priests, Levites, and temple servants are listed separately from the general population of the returning exiles and only after the other people are listed?

_____

_____

_____

The listing in 2:3-35 of the returning exiles who were not priests or other clergy is in two parts. Those included in the first part (verses 3-20) are listed according to family names; those included in the second part (verses 21-35) are listed by town.

16. In the listing by family name in 2:3-20, which two family groups were the largest, and how many did each of those two groups include? Also, which group was the smallest, and how many did it have?

_____

17. In the listing by town in 2:21-35, which group was the largest, and how many did it include? Which three groups were the smallest, and how many did each of those three groups have?

_____

_____

_____

_____

The priests (2:36). "The laity [see 2:2-35] are mentioned ahead of the clergy [see 2:36-58], in keeping with the emphasis in Ezra and Nehemiah on the significance of the common people in rebuilding the kingdom."[8]

The Levites (2:40). "The number of Levites is surprisingly low compared to the priests."[9] "Since the Levites had been entrusted with the menial tasks of temple service, many of them may have found a more comfortable way of life in exile."[10]

The musicians (2:41). In 1 Chronicles 6:31-32 and 15:16, note how the duties of musicians were described in the time of David.

The gatekeepers (2:42). See how their history and duties are described in 1 Chronicles 9:17-27. In the time of Moses and Joshua, the zealous hero Phinehas was in charge of the gatekeepers (9:20).

Descendants of the servants of Solomon (2:58). These apparently also served in the temple, although little is known about them.

18. What is the significance of the actions taken in 2:59-63 toward the people listed there?

_____

_____

25

_____

_____

_____

"This list of exiles who returned may not appear theologically important, but the repetition of the same list, with some variations, in Nehemiah 7 would suggest otherwise. First, the Lord knows His people personally. The covenant relation between the Lord and His people is a bond of intimate friendship. Second, common people are vital to the accomplishing of God's redemptive plan. Not only are the religious and political leaders important in rebuilding the house of God, but so are the common people.... Third, the enumeration resembles those found in Numbers and Joshua (Numbers 1; 26; Joshua 18; 19). As the Lord formed the covenant community following the Exodus from Egypt, so He re-creates it following the return from Babylon."[11]

Urim and Thummim (2:63). These were objects placed in or on the high priest's breastpiece (see Exodus 28:30) and were used in some way to discern God's will, possibly as a form of casting lots (see Numbers 27:21; Deuteronomy 33:8; 1 Samuel 14:41; 28:6).

The whole company numbered 42,360 (2:64). This is more than the sum of the figures given throughout the list in 2:3-60. It may be that the list includes only those from Judah and Benjamin, while the larger number includes returning exiles from the other tribes of Israel.

19. What does 2:68-69 indicate about the people's attitude toward the temple, which still had not been rebuilt?

_____

_____

_____

Settled in their own towns (2:70). "Later Nehemiah would be compelled to move people by lot to reinforce the population of Jerusalem, as the capital city had suffered the severest loss of life at the time of the Babylonian attacks. The survivors, who came for the most part from towns in the countryside, naturally preferred to resettle in their hometowns."[12]

Worship Reborn

Read again through all of Ezra 3.

20. Why do you think the returning exiles chose first to rebuild the altar?

_____

_____

_____

21. Outline and summarize the actions taken by the people in 3:1-7.

_____

_____

_____

_____

Began the work (3:8). They had made a beginning, which is, of course, the first requirement in completing any task or project.

For Thought and Discussion: For the people now gathered in Jerusalem (see 3:1), what kind of sensory perceptions would be experienced as the sacrificing of burnt offerings was renewed on the rebuilt altar (see 3:3-6)? What would they see, hear, smell, and feel?

22. Think about the crucial factors involved in getting the temple rebuilt. What were the things that had to happen before this project could be started?

_____

_____

_____

_____

23. Summarize what the people accomplished in 3:8-13.

_____

_____

_____

_____

24. What various emotions were displayed over the accomplishment, and how would you explain what caused these emotions?

_____

_____

_____

_____

25. In these three opening chapters of Ezra, what is the best evidence you see of God's sovereign control over all circumstances? How is this fact emphasized in these chapters?

_____

_____

_____

_____

_____

26. What evidence of teamwork and leadership among God's people do you see in these chapters?

_____

_____

_____

Shouted for joy . . . shouts of joy (3:12-13). They "shouted for joy at the tops of their voices."[13] "Loud shouting . . . expresses great jubilation or intense purpose (cf. 10:12; Joshua 6:5,20; 1 Samuel 4:5; Psalm 95:1-2)."[14]

"In Ezra 3 we see that the service of God requires a united effort (verse 1), leadership (verse 2a), obedience to God's Word (verse 2b), courage in the face of opposition (verse 3), offerings and funds (verses 4-7), and an organized division of labor (verses 8-9). Meeting these requirements would result in a sound foundation for later work (verse 11), tears and joy (verses 11-12), and praise and thanksgiving to the Lord (verse 11)."[15]

27. What would you select as the key verse or passage in Ezra 1–3—one that best captures or reflects the dynamics of what these chapters are all about?

_____

_____

28. List any lingering questions you have about Ezra 1–3.

_____

_____

_____

_____

For the Group

In your first meeting, it may be helpful to turn to the front of this book and review together the "How to Use This Guide" section.

You may want to focus your discussion for lesson 1 on the following issues, themes, and concepts. These things will likely reflect what group members have learned in their individual study of this week's passage, although they'll have made discoveries in other areas as well.

- God's sovereign control over history
- God's discipline and training of His people
- How God works through all His people
- The importance of corporate worship for God's people
- Working together for the Lord

The following numbered questions in lesson 1 may stimulate your best and most helpful discussion: 4, 10, 12, 20, 22, 23, 24, 25, and 27.

Look also at the questions in the margin under the heading "For Thought and Discussion."

1. *ESV Study Bible* (Wheaton, IL: Crossway, 2008), on Ezra 1:1.
2. J. S. Wright, "Ezra," in *The New Bible Dictionary*, ed. J. D. Douglas (Grand Rapids, MI: Eerdmans, 1962), 409.
3. *New Geneva Study Bible* (Nashville: Thomas Nelson, 1995), introduction to Ezra, "Characteristics and Themes."
4. F. Charles Fensham, *The Books of Ezra and Nehemiah* (Grand Rapids, MI: Eerdmans, 1982), 24–25.
5. Edwin M. Yamauchi, *Ezra-Nehemiah*, in vol. 4 of *The Expositor's Bible Commentary*, ed. Frank E. Gabelein (Grand Rapids, MI: Zondervan, 1990), 635.
6. C. F. Keil, *Ezra, Nehemiah, Esther*, vol. 4, in C. F. Keil and F. Delitzsch, *Commentary on the Old Testament* (Peabody, MA: Hendrickson, n.d.; original edition published by T. & T. Clark, Edinburgh, U.K., 1866–1891), 5.
7. *International Standard Bible Encyclopedia*, vol. 4 (Grand Rapids, MI: Eerdmans, 1988), 1194.

8. *New Geneva Study Bible*, on Ezra 2:2-35.
9. *ESV Study Bible*, on Ezra 2:36-58.
10. *NIV Study Bible* (Grand Rapids, MI: Zondervan, 1985), on Ezra 2:40.
11. *New Geneva Study Bible*, on Ezra 2:1-70.
12. Yamauchi, 621.
13. *Revised English Bible* (London: Oxford and Cambridge, 1989), on Ezra 3:12.
14. Yamauchi, 625.
15. Yamauchi, 590.

EZRA 4–6

Learning to Overcome

The elders of the Jews continued to build and prosper.... They finished building the temple according to the command of the God of Israel and the decrees of Cyrus, Darius and Artaxerxes, kings of Persia.

EZRA 6:14

"Ezra 4:6-23 must be regarded as parenthetical. . . . Thus chapter 4 is not meant to be in chronological sequence; rather it supplies us with a logical thought pattern wherein the most important actions of the Samaritans against the Jews are enumerated. In verse 24 the author comes back to his chronological sequence, interrupted by 4:6-23."[1]

Timeline for Chapter 4
• 4:1-5—events under Persia's King Cyrus (539–530 BC)
• 4:6—events under Xerxes (485–465)
• 4:7-23—events under Artaxerxes I (464–424)
• 4:24 reverts to the time of Darius I (522–486), when the temple was completed

For Thought and
Discussion: The lead-
ers of God's people
spurned the offer
from their enemies
to help rebuild the
temple. Look at how
they responded to
this offer in 4:3. Does
this in any way reflect
unwise narrowness
and closed-minded-
ness on the part of
the Jewish leaders?

Loss of Momentum

Quickly read through all of Ezra 4.

1. Summarize the developments taking place in chapter 4, using the timeline on page 33 to help you.

   _____

   _____

   _____

2. What significance do you see in the interchange mentioned in 4:1-3—especially in Zerubbabel's response?

   _____

   _____

   _____

   _____

Enemies (4:1). For further background on these people, see 2 Kings 17:24-41.

Xerxes (4:6). Or, in the Hebrew here, Ahasuerus. This is also the name he has in the Hebrew in the book of Esther.

Written . . . in the Aramaic language (4:7). At this point, the original language in Ezra changes from Hebrew to Aramaic. The Hebrew resumes in 6:19 and continues to the end. "Aramaic . . . had been the official imperial language under the Babylonians and was still used in diplomacy."[2]

3. Review the letter included in 4:11-16.

   a. What is the current situation they describe?

   _____

   _____

b. What potential future development do they warn about?

_____

_____

c. How do they characterize the Jews and Jerusalem?

_____

_____

d. What do they request the king to do?

_____

_____

Rebuilding that rebellious and wicked city . . . restoring the walls and repairing the foundations (4:12). "From the contents of the letter it is clear that work on the wall of Jerusalem and in the city itself is meant. Some time before Nehemiah had succeeded with his request, the Jews started rebuilding the wall and the ruins of Jerusalem."[3]

---

4. Summarize the substance of the king's response as seen in 4:17-22.

_____

_____

_____

_____

5. What was the effect of the king's response as seen in 4:23-24?

_____

_____

_____

For Thought and Discussion: Is it true that doing God's work will always bring worldly opposition?

Optional Application: Earlier, the people had "made a beginning" (Ezra 3:8, ESV), but then, facing severe opposition, eventually "the work . . . came to a standstill" (4:24). In your own life, are there any important and necessary tasks that have been begun but are now at a standstill because of various difficulties or opposition? If so, what needs to be the next step, from God's perspective?

For Thought and Discussion: Keeping in mind the example of Haggai and Zechariah in 5:1-2, in what endeavors today do you think the people of God need "support" from "the prophets of God"?

"Ezra 4 teaches that doing the work of God brings opposition. . . . Far from being discouraged, however, we need to be alert and vigorous, knowing that by God's grace we can triumph over all opposition and accomplish his will with rejoicing (6:14-16)."[4]

The Plot Thickens

Now read through all of Ezra 5 again.

6. From what you see in Ezra 5:1-2, what were the most important factors for putting back on track the rebuilding of the temple?

_____

_____

_____

_____

7. How does the prophet Haggai describe the condition of the temple in Haggai 1:4 and 1:9?

_____

_____

_____

8. "Then Zerubbabel . . . and Joshua . . . set to work to rebuild the house of God in Jerusalem. And the prophets of God were with them, supporting them" (Ezra 5:2). In the space provided, summarize how the prophets supported these men as evidenced in the prophets' writings.

in Haggai 1–2

_____

_____

in Zechariah 3–4

_____

_____

9. Summarize the nature and significance of Tattenai's interest in the temple's rebuilding as revealed in 5:3-5.

_____

_____

_____

_____

10. Examine Tattenai's letter to King Darius in 5:6-17.

a. How does he represent the current situation in Jerusalem (see verse 8)?

_____

_____

b. What questions and challenges does he say were given to the Jews (see verses 9-10)?

_____

_____

c. What response from the Jews does he report (see verses 11-16)?

_____

_____

d. What request does Tattenai make of the king (see verse 17)?

_____

_____

For Further Study:
How would you compare the planned dimensions and description of this temple as stated in Ezra 6:4 with the descriptions you see of Solomon's temple in 1 Kings 6?

Let It Be Done

Read through all of Ezra 6 again.

11. Chapter 6 has been called the key to the book of Ezra. Why might this be so?

_____

_____

12. Summarize the contents of the scroll found in Ecbatana, as recorded in 6:2-5.

_____

_____

_____

13. How do the contents of the record in 6:2-5 differ from the proclamation made by King Cyrus in chapter 1?

_____

_____

_____

14. Examine the decree of King Darius given in 6:6-12.

a. What does Darius authorize the Jews in Jerusalem to do?

_____

_____

b. What support does he give them?

_____

_____

c. What protection does he give them?

_____

_____

d. What does this decree indicate about Darius's understanding, attitudes, and beliefs regarding the Lord God?

_____

_____

"The king's positive attitude toward the Jews and Judah must be interpreted not only as continuing the policy of Cyrus, but also as being politically expedient for the king. Egypt was conquered only in 523 BC, and it was necessary to have loyal subjects so close to Egypt, which was always a difficult country to dominate."[5]

15. What is important to note about the response to Darius's decree as recorded in 6:13-22?

_____

_____

_____

16. What clues do you see in 6:13-15 for why the Jews were successful in rebuilding the temple?

_____

_____

_____

_____

The elders of the Jews continued to build (6:14). Work resumed on the temple in 520 BC.

For Thought and Discussion: What is the full significance of the fact that while the temple was so important to God's people and their worship in Old Testament times, the people of God have no such temple today?

17. Look again at God's words in Haggai 2:1-5 regarding the work of rebuilding the temple at this time. What reason for the people's dismay did He point to, and what encouragement—and reasons for it—did He offer?

_____

_____

_____

They finished building the temple (6:14). The year was 516 BC. This temple, though smaller than Solomon's temple, would later be dramatically enlarged by Herod the Great into the great temple complex that existed in New Testament times.

Artaxerxes (6:14). "The inclusion here of Artaxerxes I, who ruled after the events of this chapter, anticipates his decree in support of Ezra's mission (7:11-26)."[6] "The reference could be a preview to the finishing of the rebuilding of the entire 'house of God,' including the community and the wall that were rebuilt under the authority of Artaxerxes I (7:11-26; Nehemiah 2:1,8)."[7]

18. In chapters 4–6 of Ezra, what is the best evidence you see of God's sovereign control over all circumstances? How is this fact emphasized in these chapters?

_____

_____

_____

_____

19. What would you select as the key verse or passage in Ezra 4–6—one that best captures or reflects the dynamics of what these chapters are all about?

_____

_____

20. List any lingering questions you have about
    Ezra 4–6.

    _____

    _____

    _____

For the Group

Remember to pray together about your decisions for
application. Consider holding one another account-
able for those decisions, and help each other in
whatever creative ways you can.

　　You may want to focus your discussion for lesson 2 especially on the following issues, themes,
and concepts. These will likely reflect what group
members have learned in their individual study of
this week's passage, although they'll have made discoveries in other areas as well.

- Responding to and overcoming opposition
- Endurance and patience
- God's sovereignty
- Worship and celebration
- Salvation and deliverance

　　The following numbered questions in lesson 2
may stimulate your best and most helpful discussion: 6, 8, 11, 15, 16, 17, 18, and 20.
　　Look also at the questions in the margin under
the heading "For Thought and Discussion."

1. F. Charles Fensham, *The Books of Ezra and Nehemiah*
   (Grand Rapids, MI: Eerdmans, 1982), 77.
2. *ESV Study Bible* (Wheaton, IL: Crossway, 2008), on Ezra
   4:7-8.
3. Fensham, 72.
4. Edwin M. Yamauchi, *Ezra-Nehemiah*, in vol. 4 of *The
   Expositor's Bible Commentary*, ed. Frank E. Gabelein
   (Grand Rapids, MI: Zondervan, 1990), 590–591.
5. Fensham, 13.
6. *ESV Study Bible*, on Ezra 6:14.
7. *New Geneva Study Bible* (Nashville: Thomas Nelson, 1995),
   on Ezra 6:14.

EZRA 7–8

A Man of God's Word

Ezra had devoted himself to the study and observance of the Law of the LORD, and to teaching its decrees and laws in Israel.

EZRA 7:10

1. Proverbs 2:1-5 tells about the sincere person who truly longs for wisdom and understanding and who searches the Scriptures for it as if there were treasure buried there. Such a person, this passage says, will come to understand the fear of the Lord and discover the knowledge of God. As you continue exploring the book of Ezra, what "hidden treasure" would you like God to help you find here to show you what God and His wisdom are really like? If you have this desire, how would you express it in your own words of prayer to God?

_____

_____

_____

_____

_____

_____

_____

Leader and Teacher

Read through all of Ezra 7 again.

After these things (7:1). More than a half century separates the close of Ezra 6 from the beginning of Ezra 7.

During the reign of Artaxerxes king of Persia (7:1). He ruled from 465 to 424 BC. See Nehemiah 2:1; 5:14; 13:6. Artaxerxes I was the son of Xerxes I (Ahasuerus), who was king in the book of Esther.

---

2. In Ezra 7, what do you learn about the following aspects of Ezra's personality?

   his vocation

   _____

   _____

   his character

   _____

   _____

   his motives

   _____

   _____

"Ezra is the central character in this story of starting over. He is a decisive character whose arrival with the second wave of returnees causes sparks to fly."[1]

3. What do you see as most significant in the long lineage of Ezra as summarized in 7:1-5?

   _____

   _____

_____

_____

The son of Zadok (7:2). The name means "righteous." Ezra's ancestor Zadok was noted for his loyalty and faithful service to David (see 2 Samuel 15:24-37; 17:15-16; 1 Kings 1:8,26,32-45; 2:35; 1 Chronicles 15:11-15; 16:39-40; 24:1-4). The prophet Ezekiel, in his vision of the new temple, foresaw an even more exalted ministry for Zadok's descendants because of their demonstrated faithfulness.

The son of Phinehas, the son of Eleazar, the son of Aaron the chief priest (7:5). Ezra was descended from the most exalted lineage in the priesthood. Phinehas was particularly noted for his zeal at a crucial time in Israel's history (see Numbers 25). In a genealogy given in 1 Chronicles 9, this notation is added to his name: "The LORD was with him" (verse 20).

_____

4. How are Ezra's qualifications described in 7:6, and what is the significance of these qualifications in light of the ministry Ezra has in the rest of the book of Ezra and in Nehemiah 8?

_____

_____

_____

_____

_____

_____

_____

A teacher (7:6). Or "scribe," as in most English versions. In the books of Ezra and Nehemiah, Ezra is often called "priest," "teacher," and "scribe," frequently with two of those terms together

For Further Study:
Explore how the descendants of Zadok are commended in the prophecies of Ezekiel 40:44-46, 43:18-19, 44:15-31, and 48:10-12. How does God view their faithfulness, and how does it compare with Ezra's faithfulness?

For Further Study:
What do you learn about Phinehas, the illustrious ancestor of Ezra, in these passages: Numbers 25; Joshua 22:30-33; 1 Chronicles 9:20; Psalm 106:30-31. In what ways does the character of Phinehas match that of Ezra?

Optional Application: In what ways does God want you to be "skilled" in His Word, as Ezra was (7:6, ESV)?

For Thought and Discussion: Do you think Ezra is the kind of person you would have enjoyed being around? If so, for what reasons?

(see 7:11-12,21; 10:10; Nehemiah 8:2,4,9,13; 12:26,36).

Well versed in the Law of Moses (7:6). Or "skilled in the Law of Moses," as in most English versions. "Well versed *(māhîr)* is a word that literally means 'quick' or 'swift.' It occurs in only three other passages: Psalm 45:1, 'a skillful writer'; Proverbs 22:29, 'skilled in his work'; and Isaiah 16:5, 'speeds the cause of righteousness.'"[2]

The hand of the LORD his God was on him (7:6). See the same or similar phrasing in 7:9, 7:28, 8:18, 8:22, and 8:31. The phrase "a striking expression of God's favor"[3] is also used of Nehemiah (see Nehemiah 2:8).

"Ezra experienced the good hand of God. . . . He believed that God could guide and protect from misfortune (8:20-22). As an inspired leader he enlisted others and assigned trustworthy men to their tasks (7:27-28; 8:15,24). He regarded what he did as a sacred trust (8:21-28)."[4]

5. What significance do you see in the kinds of people who are listed in 7:7 as among those returning to Jerusalem?

_____

_____

_____

_____

6. In Ezra 7 and 8, what specific difference in Ezra's life is stated as the result of God's hand being upon him, and what is the significance of this (see especially 7:6,9,28 and 8:18,22,31)?

_____

_____

_____

_____

_____

"It is only the gracious hand of God that enables a man or a woman to fulfill his or her calling in ministry. It is the hand of God that gives courage for spiritual leadership, humility for corporate repentance, and wisdom for teaching God's Word. Praise God for the hand of guidance that has brought you to your present place of service, for the hand of providence that will supply all your needs, for the hand of discipline that will train you in righteousness, and for the hand of comfort that will sustain you through trials. The hand of God is on you for blessing."[5]

For Further Study:
How does the fact and concept of God's hand being upon someone relate to the biblical truths taught in these passages: Psalm 25:8-9; 32:8; Proverbs 3:6; 16:9; Isaiah 30:20-21; 48:17; Jeremiah 10:23; James 1:5.

Optional Application: In your life, what does it mean—or what could it mean—for the hand of the Lord to be upon you, as it was for Ezra?

Ezra had devoted himself (7:10). Literally, "set his heart." "Ezra thus concentrated his whole life on the study of the law. But it is not only a question of study, he also practiced the law. It was not a dead letter, but a living reality to him."[6] "Bible study was not merely an intellectual discipline but a personal study for his own life and for the instruction of his congregation."[7] It was because of this very quality in Ezra that "the gracious hand of his God was on him" (7:9). "The hand of his God graciously arranged for him, for he had prepared his heart to seek and to do the law of Jahve, i.e., to make the law of God his rule of action."[8]

47

For Further Study:
From Ezra 7:10, we see that Ezra was not only a committed student of God's Word but also a committed teacher. How do you see that commitment as a biblical teacher played out in Nehemiah 8?

For Thought and Discussion: In comparison to God's people in Old Testament times, should the written Word of God be *more* important for us than it was for them, *less* important, or of *equal* importance? Explain your answer.

Optional Application: Look again at Ezra's devotion to studying and obeying the Scriptures as mentioned in 7:10. How strongly does this reflect your own attitude toward the Scriptures?

7. What would you suggest are the underlying factors that motivated Ezra to demonstrate the kind of commitment to the Lord's Word described in 7:10?

_____

_____

_____

"The logic of [Ezra 7:10] is impeccable. There were three things that Ezra was committed to doing, and he had them in the proper order, like 'A-B-C' or '1-2-3.' In fact, Ezra had them in the only order that makes any sense: he had his heart set on studying, doing, and teaching the Word of God. This was his heart commitment, the direction of his life, the settled intention of his soul."[9]

8. On Ezra's part, what thoughts, emotions, and choices would likely be represented by what is stated about him in 7:10?

_____

_____

_____

9. In drawing attention to Ezra's commitment to Scripture, Ezra 7:10 uses three terms to describe God's Word—"the Law of the LORD," "decrees," and "laws." Notice the similar manifold terminology for God's Word in one of the classic biblical proclamations of the glory and preciousness of Scripture, Psalm 19:7-11. Study this passage and use its truth to describe the value and power of the Word of God to which Ezra was so committed.

_____

_____

_____

_____

10. Summarize the contents of the letter from King Artaxerxes to Ezra as recorded in 7:11-26.

_____

_____

_____

_____

a. How did he refer to Ezra, and what is significant about this?

_____

_____

b. What exactly did he allow or request Ezra to do?

_____

_____

c. What did he allow other people to do?

_____

_____

d. In what ways did he give latitude to Ezra in his actions?

_____

_____

e. What did he command his royal treasuries across the empire to do?

_____

_____

Optional Application: Ezra's commitment to God's Word was a core factor in his mission and calling in life. "He had made the investigation of the law, for the sake of introducing the practice of the same among the congregation, his life-task."[10] How does your own commitment to God's Word relate to your life-task and life-calling?

Optional Application: As these events unfolded, Ezra used them as an opportunity to praise his God in 7:27-28. What praise is due to God from you for the things He has recently brought about in your own life?

For Further Study: Ezra recognizes that God has sovereignly arranged events that would "beautify" or "bring honor to" the temple in Jerusalem as the house of the Lord (see 7:27). Look at the promise God makes in the last sentence in Isaiah 60:7. What purposes do you think God has in mind in wanting to "adorn" or "beautify" or "honor" His temple?

f. In what ways did the king acknowledge God in his letter?

_____

_____

g. How did he link his own decrees with those of God?

_____

_____

h. What punishment did he set down for those who disobeyed his laws or God's?

_____

_____

11. What is noteworthy in Ezra's response to this letter as we see it in 7:27-28?

_____

_____

_____

_____

To bring honor to the house of the LORD (7:27). Literally, "to beautify the house of the LORD" (ESV). "Ezra names the beautifying of the house of God as the occasion of his thanksgiving . . . because the re-establishment of divine worship was the re-establishment of the moral and religious life of the community."[11]

The Return

Read through all of Ezra 8 again.

12. From Ezra 8, outline and summarize the specific actions taken by Ezra in leading this new group of exiles to Jerusalem.

_____

_____

_____

_____

13. What observations and conclusions from Ezra 8 can you provide about Ezra's leadership style and abilities?

_____

_____

_____

14. What more do you learn about Ezra's heart and character from the events described in chapter 8?

_____

_____

_____

15. In 8:15-20, what significance do you see in Ezra's determined effort to find Levites to join them in returning to Jerusalem?

_____

_____

_____

_____

I proclaimed a fast, so that we might humble ourselves before our God (8:21). "Fasting was accompanied by prayer. The prayer here was a humble supplication to God to assist them on their journey, especially since whole families were returning. . . . In these verses it is obvious that Ezra was sensitive to the imminent danger which confronted him. Ezra acted in faith and relied totally on the Lord for the outcome of his journey."[12]

For Further Study:
"Fasting, as a means of humbling themselves before God, for the purpose of obtaining an answer to their petitions, was an ancient custom with the Israelites."[13] What can you discover about this from these passages: Judges 20:26; 1 Samuel 7:6; 2 Chronicles 20:3; Esther 4:15-16; Joel 1:14.

For Thought and Discussion: Because of the people's stated dependence on God's protection, Ezra said he "was ashamed" to ask the king for military protection for the journey to Jerusalem. Note that later, Nehemiah had a military escort of officers and cavalry when he returned to Jerusalem (see Nehemiah 2:9) and apparently had no qualms about this. How would you compare the two situations? Was either of the two men lacking in faith or wisdom? Explain your answers.

And he answered our prayer (8:23). This statement looks ahead to their safe journey's completion in 8:32.

16. What is significant in Ezra's instructions to the leading priests in 8:28-29?

_____

_____

_____

_____

We arrived in Jerusalem (8:32). Their journey of approximately nine hundred miles lasted almost four months.

We rested three days (8:32). This is similar to what Nehemiah will do after his journey to Jerusalem (see Nehemiah 2:11). "They remained . . . quiet and inactive three days, to recover from the fatigues and hardships of the journey, before they undertook the arrangement of their affairs."[14]

17. What is noteworthy about the actions taken by the newly returned exiles in 8:35-36?

_____

_____

_____

_____

Burnt offerings . . . twelve bulls for all Israel (8:35). "For these exiles it is a first chance to see and worship at the rebuilt temple, and their sacrifices resemble those made at its first dedication (see 6:16-17)."[15] "The fact that these were offered for all Israel was an actual declaration that they who had now returned were henceforth resolved, together with all Israel, to dedicate their lives to the service of the Lord their God."[16]

Optional Application: What need is there for fasting in your own life, especially as a way to humble yourself before the Lord and to seek His protection, as we see in Ezra's example?

18. In chapters 7–8 of Ezra, what is the best evidence you see of God's sovereign control over all circumstances? How is this fact emphasized in these chapters?

_____

_____

_____

_____

19. What would you select as the key verse or passage in Ezra 7–8—one that best captures or reflects the dynamics of what these chapters are all about?

_____

_____

20. List any lingering questions you have about Ezra 7–8.

_____

_____

_____

_____

For the Group

Consider praying together for continuing discernment in applying these chapters to your lives.

You may want to focus your discussion for lesson 3 especially on the following issues, themes, and concepts. These will likely reflect what group members have learned in their individual study of this week's passage, although they'll have made discoveries in other areas as well.

- Devotion and obedience to God's Word
- Teaching God's Word

- Godly leadership
- God's sovereignty
- Courage
- Dependence on God

The following numbered questions in lesson 3 may stimulate your best and most helpful discussion: 2, 7, 11, 12, 13, 14, and 19.

Remember to look also at the "Thought and Discussion" questions in the margin.

1. *ESV Study Bible* (Wheaton, IL: Crossway, 2008), introduction to Ezra, "Literary Features."
2. Edwin M. Yamauchi, *Ezra-Nehemiah*, in vol. 4 of *The Expositor's Bible Commentary*, ed. Frank E. Gabelein (Grand Rapids, MI: Zondervan, 1990), 649.
3. Yamauchi, 650.
4. Yamauchi, 591.
5. Philip Graham Ryken, "Ezra, According to the Gospel: Ezra 7:10," in *Themelios: An International Journal for Pastors and Students of Theological and Religious Studies*, vol. 33, issue 3 (December 2008), 64.
6. F. Charles Fensham, *The Books of Ezra and Nehemiah* (Grand Rapids, MI: Eerdmans, 1982), 101.
7. Yamauchi, 650.
8. C. F. Keil, *Ezra, Nehemiah, Esther*, vol. 4, in C. F. Keil and F. Delitzsch, *Commentary on the Old Testament* (Peabody, MA: Hendrickson, n.d.; original edition published by T. & T. Clark, Edinburgh, U.K., 1866–1891), 60–61.
9. Ryken, 65.
10. Keil, 60.
11. Keil, 64.
12. Fensham, 116.
13. Keil, 68.
14. Keil, 70.
15. *ESV Study Bible*, on Ezra 8:35.
16. Keil, 71.

EZRA 9–10

A Crisis of Unfaithfulness

LORD, the God of Israel, you are righteous! We are left this day as a remnant. Here we are before you in our guilt, though because of it not one of us can stand in your presence.

EZRA 9:15

1. What do these chapters reveal about Ezra's character and his spiritual condition?

_____

_____

_____

_____

_____

2. From what you see in these chapters, what are the most important things Ezra understands about God's personality and character?

_____

_____

_____

_____

_____

For Thought and Discussion: Was Ezra in any way overre-acting when he felt "ashamed and dis-graced" (9:6) before God because of the people's intermar-riage with foreign-ers? Is that the way *we* should feel when there is significant sin in the body of believ-ers of which we are a part?

For Further Study: Explore the concept of the "holy seed" or "holy offspring" as seen in Isaiah 6:13. Recognize also how it is implicit in God's promises to Abraham in Genesis 12:1-3, 15:5, and 17:7-8 (see also Galatians 3:16). What observations and conclusions can you make about this idea of the "holy seed"?

Optional Application: When you consider how Israel's mingling with foreign wives is spo-ken against in Ezra 9–10, what might this sin correspond to in the lives of Christians today? What might it correspond to in your own life? In regard to this, what confession before God is needed in your life?

A Reason for Distress

Quickly read through all of Ezra 9 again.

3. What exactly did Ezra learn in 9:1-2?

_____

_____

After these things . . . the leaders came to me and said (9:1). "Ezra may have received the information concerning the unlawful mar-riages, not during the month of his arrival at Jerusalem, but some months later. We are not told whether it was given immediately, or soon after the completion of the matters mentioned in 8:33-36."[1]

This unfaithfulness (9:2). "The author clearly emphasized the gravity of the sin which was committed. The law of God must be kept, and any transgression of this law was regarded as serious."[2]

4. Compare the list of nations mentioned in 9:1 with those named in Exodus 34:11-16 and Deuteronomy 7:1-5. According to these pas-sages, how did God want the people of Israel to deal with these nations?

_____

_____

The holy race (9:2). Literally, "holy seed."

5. According to 9:3-6, what was Ezra's response to this information he received? Why do you think he responded this way?

_____

_____

_____

_____

Everyone who trembled at the words of the God of Israel (9:4). See also 10:3.

6. How would you outline the contents of Ezra's prayer in 9:6-15? What do you believe are the most significant elements in his prayer?

_____

_____

_____

_____

_____

_____

Optional Application: What need is there in your own life to "tremble at the words of God"? In prayer, speak honestly with Him about this.

The Lord our God has been gracious. . . . Our God has not forsaken us. . . . He has shown us kindness. . . . He has granted us new life (9:8-9). "God . . . is the God of history, and his will is revealed through the historical process. . . . Everything that happened in the past to Israel is interpreted as the will of God; their moments of decline and their moments of success are ascribed to his will. . . . Hence, the Lord not only determined the history of his own people, but also fulfills his will through the mighty kings of foreign nations."[3]

7. How does the situation Ezra describes in his prayer (see 9:6-15) compare to our own condition as sinners before God and our need for the gospel of Christ? In particular, to what extent do Ezra's words in 9:8-9 reflect the grace we have received in the gospel of Christ?

_____

_____

Optional Application: What elements of Ezra's prayer in 9:6-15 are appropriate elements in your own prayer in light of how you're doing today in your life and in your relationship with God?

"One must keep in mind that the Jews were at that moment in history the carriers of the Lord's revelation. Contamination of their religion with foreign elements, which could alter considerably the orthodox conceptions, was regarded as such a danger that everything possible was done to combat it. . . .

"Once they had conceded on certain points, it would become more and more difficult to keep up the principles of their own religion. The next step would be to become so familiar and associate on such a friendly footing with foreigners that intermarriage became possible. The danger of this development was grasped fully by Ezra and Nehemiah. Once intermarriage was allowed, the purity of the religion of the Lord would be in jeopardy, because of the potential influence of foreigners on the children of such marriages.

"Therefore, strong-minded leaders like Ezra and Nehemiah were necessary to take stern measures to protect the purity of the religion."[4]

Giving us a firm place in his sanctuary (9:8). Literally, a "peg" or "nail" in the place of His sanctuary. "The expression is figurative. . . . Such a nail was the place of God's sanctuary, the temple, to the rescued community. This was to

them a firm nail, by which they were borne and
upheld; and this nail God had given them as
a support to which they might cling, and gain
new life and vigor."[5]

The Way of Repentance

Read through the last chapter of Ezra again.

"Prayer is woven thoroughly into the
fabric of these two books [Ezra and
Nehemiah]. It takes a variety of forms,
from a momentary flash of mental prayer
to an eloquent address, accompanied on
a penitential occasion by such outward
gestures as fasting, pulling out the hair,
rending the garments, weeping, casting
oneself down (cf. Ezra 9:3; 10:1), or
wearing sackcloth and putting earth on
one's head (Nehemiah 9:1); or again, on
a joyful occasion reinforcing praise with
the music and shouts of acclamation. . . .

"In their content the prayers reflect
a mature Old Testament faith. There is
a strong sense of history and of Israelite
solidarity, not only where this is reassuring
by virtue of election and covenant and
the memory of redemption (Nehemiah
9:7-15), but equally where it is humiliating.
Ezra blushes (Ezra 9:6) for the guilt of the
present and the past, although he has
had no obvious personal share in either;
likewise Nehemiah's general confession
'we have sinned' is immediately person-
alized: 'Yea, I and my father's house have
sinned' (Nehemiah 1:6); and there is no
excuse offered."[6]

For Thought and Discussion: What principles for confession and repentance of sin do you see in chapter 10 that would be appropriate for God's people today?

While Ezra was praying and confessing (10:1). This is a characteristic of both Ezra and Nehemiah.

8. How would you summarize the response of the people as indicated in Ezra 10, and what do you think motivated their response?

_____

_____

_____

_____

9. What is especially significant in the words spoken to Ezra by Shecaniah in 10:2-4?

_____

_____

_____

10. What would have been the basis for the hope Shecaniah expressed in 10:2?

_____

_____

Let us make a covenant before our God (10:3). This reflects a profound emphasis in Ezra and Nehemiah on God's covenant relationship with His people.

Take courage and do it (10:4). Compare these words of Shecaniah to Ezra with God's words to Joshua.

11. What is significant about Ezra's further response to this crisis in 10:6?

_____

_____

60

_____

_____

"The religion of the Lord is a way of life and a living reality that grows out of a living relationship with the Lord. Ezra and Nehemiah were the first to set the example. Their prayers to the Lord give evidence of a realization of their relationship with the Lord and the acceptance that only through him could their ideals be fulfilled.

"Thus it is not surprising that the covenant relationship is so heavily stressed in the memoirs of both Ezra and Nehemiah. The covenant was the vehicle that had given expression to the relationship between the Lord and his people since the time of the patriarchs. Before and during the Exile the covenant idea was more fully worked out, especially by Jeremiah. . . . The covenant relationship was clearly a living relationship, and the prescriptions of this covenant had to be kept in everyday life."[7]

For Further Study: The concept of God's covenant relationship with His people was developed further in prophecies given through Jeremiah and Ezekiel in the century before Ezra's time (Jeremiah in approximately 626–585 BC, and Ezekiel in 593–571). From what the following passages say about God's covenant with His people, how might this have influenced Ezra's mindset and ministry? Read Jeremiah 31:27-40; 32:36-44; 50:4-5; Ezekiel 11:16-21; 16:59-63; 34:25-31; 36:24-38; 37:24-28.

For Further Study: Shecaniah urged Ezra to "take courage and do it" (10:4). Compare this with the people's words to their leader in Joshua 1:16, and God's words to that same leader in Joshua 1:6-7 and 1:9. Why is such encouragement so valuable and necessary?

12. Summarize what was accomplished at the assembly in Jerusalem and afterward as described in 10:7-17.

_____

_____

_____

_____

Optional Application:
Prayerfully consider whether your pastor or some other church leader is someone who needs to hear from you the message to "take courage and do it." Or perhaps this is an encouragement that God is urging upon you at this time. What is it that you need to "take courage and do"?

13. What is significant about the names of the guilty persons being listed in 10:18-44? Approximately how many people are named on this list?

_____

_____

_____

14. What do you learn about God's wrath in Ezra 9–10 (see especially 10:10,14)?

_____

_____

_____

15. How does the situation presented in Ezra 9–10 relate to our condition as Christians when we sin against God?

_____

_____

_____

_____

16. What would you select as the key verse or passage in Ezra 9–10—one that best captures or reflects the dynamics of what these chapters are all about?

_____

_____

17. List any lingering questions you have about Ezra 9–10.

_____

_____

_____

Reviewing Ezra

18. Think back on all that's happened to the people of Israel in the book of Ezra. If it's true that the past is a lesson for the future, what would you say are the most important lessons for God's people today to learn from these events?

For Further Study: In what ways is the book of Ezra a fulfillment of the prophecy in Isaiah 44:24-28?

_____

_____

_____

_____

19. In Isaiah 55:10-11, God reminds us that in the same way He sends rain and snow from the sky to water the earth and nurture life, so also He sends His words to accomplish specific purposes. What would you suggest are God's primary purposes for the message of Ezra in the lives of His people today?

_____

_____

_____

_____

20. Recall the guidelines given for our thought life in Philippians 4:8: "Whatever is true, whatever is noble, whatever is right, whatever is pure, whatever is lovely, whatever is admirable—if anything is excellent or praiseworthy—think about such things." As you reflect on all you've read in the book of Ezra, what stands out to you as being particularly true, or noble, or right, or pure, or lovely, or admirable, or excellent, or praiseworthy—and therefore well worth thinking more about?

_____

_____

_____

_____

Optional Application: Which verses in Ezra would be most helpful for you to memorize so you have them always available in your mind and heart for the Holy Spirit to use?

21. Considering that all of Scripture testifies ultimately of Christ, where does Jesus come most in focus for you in this book?

_____

_____

_____

"When the Bible says that Ezra studied 'the Law of the Lord' (7:10), we understand this to refer to God's Word generally. When Ezra studied the law, he was also beginning to understand the gospel, for the grace of God and the promise of Jesus Christ are taught in Ezra as much as anywhere else in the Scriptures."[8]

22. In your understanding, what are the strongest ways in which the book of Ezra points us to mankind's need for Jesus and what He accomplished in His death and resurrection?

_____

_____

_____

_____

23. In Romans 15:4, Paul reminds us that the Old Testament Scriptures can give us patience and perseverance on one hand as well as comfort and encouragement on the other. In your own life, how do you see the book of Ezra living up to Paul's description? In what ways do they help to meet your personal needs for both perseverance and encouragement?

_____

_____

_____

_____

_____

_____

For the Group

Continue to share together the principles you've found and how you're applying them to your lives. Keep encouraging each other to persevere with past applications. Discuss any specific dilemmas that group members may be facing in their lives as they seek to be obedient to God's Word.

You may want to focus your discussion for lesson 4 especially on the following issues, themes, and concepts. These will likely reflect what group members have learned in their individual study of this week's passage, although they'll have made discoveries in other areas as well.

* Grief over sin
* Holiness, purity, and separation from the world
* Godly leadership
* Confession and repentance of sin
* God's covenant love
* Our witness to the world

The following numbered questions in lesson 4 may stimulate your best and most helpful discussion: 1, 2, 5, 6, 8, 12, 14, 15, and 17.

Allow enough discussion time to look back together and review the book of Ezra as a whole. You can use the numbered questions 18, 19, 20, 21, 22, and 23 in this lesson to help you do that.

Once more, look also at the questions in the margin under the heading "For Thought and Discussion."

1. C. F. Keil, *Ezra, Nehemiah, Esther,* vol. 4, in C. F. Keil and F. Delitzsch, *Commentary on the Old Testament* (Peabody, MA: Hendrickson, n.d.; original edition published by T. & T. Clark, Edinburgh, U.K., 1866–1891), 73.
2. F. Charles Fensham, *The Books of Ezra and Nehemiah* (Grand Rapids, MI: Eerdmans, 1982), 145.
3. Fensham, 19.
4. Fensham, 18.
5. Keil, 75.

6. Derek Kidner, *Ezra and Nehemiah: An Introduction and Commentary* (Downers Grove, IL: InterVarsity, 1979), 24–25.
7. Fensham, 17–18.
8. Philip Graham Ryken, "Ezra, According to the Gospel: Ezra 7:10," in *Themelios: An International Journal for Pastors and Students of Theological and Religious Studies,* vol. 33, issue 3 (December 2008), 67.

INTRODUCTION

THE BOOK OF NEHEMIAH

A Wall Rebuilt, a Nation Revived

About a dozen years after Ezra first returned to Jerusalem, a certain Jewish man was serving as a royal official in the court of King Artaxerxes in Susa, capital of the Persian Empire. While serving the Persian king, he received news that despite the return of thousands of Jewish exiles to Judea in recent decades, Jerusalem's wall was still in ruins and the city remained exposed to danger. That man was named Nehemiah. His response to the news of this tragedy is the subject of the book of Nehemiah.

Most of this book is taken from Nehemiah's own memoirs. It's an inspiring account of people doing God's work despite threats to their survival. It's also an instructive account of a return to faithfulness after laxity. And it provides encouraging insight into the kind of leadership required to bring these things about.

An Energetic Account

"Nehemiah's style is very much his own—simple, straightforward and business-like, yet reflecting at the same time a genuine religious zeal."[1]

"The Book of Nehemiah perhaps more than any other book of the Old Testament reflects the vibrant personality of its author."[2] "The book thrills and throbs and pulsates with the tremendous force of this man's will."[3]

In Nehemiah, "we're seeing something . . . so rare nowadays that we've hardly got a word for it. And when the regular biblical word for it is used, we hardly know what it means. That word is *zeal*. What we are watching is the action of a zealous servant of God in the face of scandalous irreverence."[4]

Nehemiah is "a servant of God, that's obvious—and a devoted one too. His service is marked by single-minded intensity. He isn't a man who lets things drift. His mind is very focused. He knows what his goals must be, and he pursues them. . . . He knows where he is going, and he takes all steps necessary to that end."[5]

Continuing from Ezra

The book of Nehemiah is intricately related to the book of Ezra (as mentioned in this guide's introduction to Ezra), and the two share common themes and purposes.

"The overall purpose of Ezra and Nehemiah is to affirm that God works sovereignly through responsible human agents to accomplish His redemptive objective."[6] "The author develops this theme in Nehemiah with particular attention to the rebuilding and dedication of the defensive walls of Jerusalem (1:1–7:3; 12:27-43) and the reconstitution of the whole people called 'Israel' in their covenant relationship with God (7:4–13:31).[7]

"The theme of Nehemiah is the Lord's protection of his people and the need for their faithfulness in keeping the Torah (the Mosaic Law) and their faithfulness in worship."[8]

1. Edwin M. Yamauchi, *Ezra-Nehemiah*, in vol. 4 of *The Expositor's Bible Commentary*, ed. Frank E. Gabelein (Grand Rapids, MI: Zondervan, 1990), 574.
2. Yamauchi, 591.
3. G. Campbell Morgan, *Living Messages of the Books of the Bible: Old Testament* (New York: Revell, 1912), 262; as quoted in Yamauchi, 591.
4. J. I. Packer, *Never Beyond Hope* (Downers Grove, IL: InterVarsity, 2000), 163.
5. Packer, 162.
6. *New Geneva Study Bible* (Nashville: Thomas Nelson, 1995), introduction to Ezra, "Characteristics and Themes."
7. *New Geneva Study Bible*, introduction to Nehemiah, "Characteristics and Themes."
8. *ESV Study Bible* (Wheaton, IL: Crossway, 2008), introduction to Nehemiah, "Theme."

NEHEMIAH 1–4

Leader and Rebuilder

*You see the trouble we are in: Jerusalem lies in
ruins, and its gates have been burned with fire.
Come, let us rebuild the wall of Jerusalem, and
we will no longer be in disgrace.*

NEHEMIAH 2:17

1. Once more, think about the encouraging guidelines in 2 Timothy 3:16-17—that *all* Scripture
   is of great benefit to (a) teach us, (b) rebuke us,
   (c) correct us, and (d) train us in righteousness, and the Scriptures will completely equip
   the person of God "for every good work." Once
   more, give serious consideration to these guidelines. In which of these areas do you especially
   want to experience the usefulness of Nehemiah?
   Express your desire in a written prayer to God.

   _____

   _____

   _____

   _____

   _____

   _____

Optional Application: Recall again how Jesus explained Old Testament passages to His disciples as He "opened their minds so they could understand the Scriptures" (Luke 24:45). Ask God to do that kind of work in *your* mind as you study Nehemiah so you're released and free to learn everything here He wants you to learn and so you can become as bold and worshipful and faithful as those early disciples of Jesus were. Express this desire to Him in prayer.

Optional Application: Does your first reading suggest ways that Nehemiah's book applies to you? If so, explain this briefly and how you might respond.

2. As you glance through the pages of Nehemiah, look for a recurring theme or thought in the following verses: 1:4; 2:4; 4:4,9; 5:19; 6:9,14; 13:14,22,29,31. What is that theme? Why is it important to God, and why is it important for all of God's people in all ages?

_____

_____

_____

_____

The best start toward understanding any book of Scripture is to read it through first for an overall sense of what the author is trying to say. Nehemiah is a captivating story and is best appreciated when read straight through for its humor, suspense, and development of plot and character. So read through the book as you would a short story. You might want to read it several times, perhaps in different translations.

3. Outline what you think are the major sections of Nehemiah. Give verse references and titles for them. Try to reduce the book to just a handful of main sections.

_____

_____

_____

_____

_____

As you continue to study Nehemiah more closely, keep in mind the big picture you've discovered.

---

4. In your initial reading of the book of Nehemiah, you may have come across concepts you'd like clarified, or you may have questions you'd like

answered as you go deeper into this study. While these thoughts are still fresh, jot down your questions here to serve as personal objectives for your investigation of this book.

_____

_____

_____

A Plea for Help

Read through Nehemiah 1 at least once before approaching the following questions.

Nehemiah (1:1). His name means "the comfort of the Lord" or "the Lord has comforted."

---

5. In 1:2-3, what was Nehemiah seeking, and what were the details of the report given to him in response?

_____

_____

_____

_____

6. In 1:4, what can we learn about Nehemiah (his character, values, and so on) from his reaction to this news?

_____

_____

_____

I sat down and wept . . . I mourned and fasted and prayed (1:4). "The religious devotion of this practical man cannot be denied."[1]

For Further Study:
Nehemiah had in mind "the exile" (1:2), an event that must surely have been deeply etched into the consciousness of the Jews. To learn more about how God's people responded to Jerusalem's destruction and the exile to Babylon, read Psalm 79 and the book of Lamentations. What are the dominant reactions that you see there?

71

7. Study Nehemiah's prayer in 1:5-11.

   a. Give a short label to each part of this prayer
      according to the sections you see it falling
      into. Write the verse reference first and then
      put your title, or label, next to it.

   _____

   _____

   b. Can you discover any elements in Nehemiah's
      prayer that you might find useful as a model
      for your own prayer life? If so, what are they
      and how might you incorporate them?

   _____

   _____

"One of the most striking characteristics
of Nehemiah was his recourse to prayer
(cf. 4:4,9; 5:19; 6:9,14; 13:14). Those who are
the boldest for God have the greatest
need to be in prayer."[2]

Covenant (1:5). The relationship between God and
   His people, the Jews. The whole history of Israel
   was the history of the covenant. It was not an
   agreement between equals but the gracious gift
   of a Sovereign to His subjects. Its main content
   was God's promises to multiply Israel, to give
   the people the land of Canaan, to protect them,
   and to make them an example to the nations
   of God's goodness. In return, the Jews were to
   fear, love, serve, and obey God alone.

Love (1:5). This is also translated as "lovingkind-
   ness" (NASB) and "steadfast love" (ESV). It is the
   attitude expected of covenanting parties toward
   one another. On God's side, it meant unfailing
   loyalty: constant provision of needs, protection
   from danger, and restoration of the nation once
   the people had repented from disobedience. It
   included forgiveness and mercy, for its essence
   was God's bending to love His creatures, even

the unrepentant. The people's response was to be "covenant love" toward God and each other.

8. List everything you observe from 1:5-11 about the character of God.

_____

_____

_____

_____

_____

For some days (1:4). The days may have stretched for months until the events recorded in chapter 2.

9. Whose sin did Nehemiah confess (see 1:6-7), and what was that sin?

_____

_____

a. Why do you think Nehemiah made this confession of sin?

_____

_____

_____

b. What does Nehemiah's prayer reveal to you about his faith?

_____

_____

_____

The instruction you gave your servant Moses (1:8). See Deuteronomy 30:1-4.

For Further Study: Why do you think Nehemiah asked God to remember His promises (see 1:8-10)?

For Further Study: To better understand Nehemiah's prayer, look up 2 Chronicles 7:14. What four things does that passage teach God's people to do? (Note especially the attitude with which they are to act.) What does this conditional promise reveal about God?

Optional Application: Are there any needs of those around you that move you as Nehemiah was moved by his people's need? What might those needs be?

For Thought and Discussion: Think about the lessons from Nehemiah's life that can be found in chapter 1. What kinds of insights and principles can you discover that apply to believers today?

Optional Application: Have you discovered a principle or insight in chapter 1 that you think God may want you to apply to your own life? If so, jot it down on a separate piece of paper, along with at least one initial step that could help you get going in this area.

Optional Application: Nehemiah prayed because he had a great burden for a specific need to carry out God's will. Can you discern a specific need for accomplishing God's purposes that God might want you to pray for? What else can you do to discover what God wants you to pray into being? What can you do to learn how He wants to use you to accomplish His ends? Try to think of a specific course of action.

In 1:10-11, Nehemiah was quoting from Deuteronomy 9:26-29. This quotation showed that he saw himself as standing "in the breach" as Moses had done (see Psalm 106:23) to save Israel through prayer. Nehemiah was acting according to the relationship he had with God; he was also responding to God's promise to all Israel in 2 Chronicles 7:14.

Redeemed (1:10). Redemption was literally a releasing from slavery or death penalty on payment of a ransom. Nehemiah was quoting Moses' use of the word in Deuteronomy 9:26, when Moses recalled how God had freed the Israelites from bondage in Egypt. In the face of a similar threat to survival, Nehemiah recalled in his prayer the act of redemption in which God had won the Israelites for Himself.

Cupbearer (1:11). "Nehemiah was a man of responsibility. That he served as the king's cupbearer (1:11–2:1) can only mean that he had proven himself trustworthy over a long period."[3]

A Risk

Read 2:1-8 before continuing with the following questions. Think about how these verses develop the themes of the book.

Nisan (2:1). April; that is, four months after the events of chapter 1.

10. According to these first eight verses of chapter 2, what was the "success" for which Nehemiah had prayed in 1:11?

_____

_____

_____

Then I prayed to the God of heaven (2:4). "Nehe-miah was a man of prayer. His first resort was to prayer (see Nehemiah 1:5-11). He prayed spontaneously even in the presence of the king (2:4-5)."[4]

"Of all biblical characters, Nehemiah is perhaps the most explicit on 'the practice of the presence of God.'"[5]

So that I can rebuild it (2:5). "Nehemiah was a man of vision. The walls of Jerusalem had been in ruins for 141 years when Nehemiah learned of an abortive attempt to rebuild them (Ezra 4:23). He had a great vision of who God was and what he could do through his servants."[6]

11. What can you tell about Nehemiah's character from his encounter with King Artaxerxes in chapter 2?

_____

_____

_____

Trans-Euphrates (2:7). This province (whose name is also translated "Beyond the River") com-prised all of Syria and Palestine. A provincial governor administered it, with district gover-nors over portions such as Samaria, Judah, and Ammon.

12. What connections between prayer and action does this passage (2:1-8) show?

_____

_____

_____

_____

For Further Study: Proverbs 21:1 asserts God's sovereignty over secular authori-ties. To further explore how God works through secu-lar governments, see Romans 13:1-7 and 1 Peter 2:12-20.

For Further Study: How does Nehemiah's strategy for dealing with his king compare to the words of Jesus in John 14:12-13?

For Thought and Discussion: Think about the risks Nehemiah took to pursue his goal. What risks do committed Christians encounter today in their work for God's kingdom? What risks might God be leading you to take in pursuing His goals? What are your resources for endur-ing these risks?

For Thought and Discussion: What can you conclude from 2:1-8 about how God works in the lives of His people (the church) or in your nation?

Optional Application:
Keep in your mind and
heart the example
of Nehemiah as a
man of prayer. Has
God revealed to
you recently any
pressing concerns
to carry before Him
in prayer—perhaps
something you dis-
covered or decided
while working
through this lesson? If
so, write down these
prayer concerns and
list a practical plan
for how you could
accomplish this task of
prayer.

To Jerusalem

Nehemiah records nothing about the dangers and
discomfort of his travel from Susa to Jerusalem.
However, we may imagine those things from the
distance involved (approximately nine hundred
miles) and from his need of an army escort (see 2:9).

*The king had also sent army officers and cav-
alry with me* (2:9). "Unlike Ezra (Ezra 8:22)
Nehemiah was accompanied by an armed
escort, not, however, because his faith was
weaker than Ezra's."[7] "Nehemiah came straight
from the court, where he had been a favorite
servant of the king, and he was now made the
official governor of Jerusalem. It was only in
accordance with custom that he should have an
escort assigned him."[8]

Sanballat (2:10). He is known from another docu-
ment to have been governor of Samaria. Until
Nehemiah was appointed, Judah had been part
of Sanballat's province.

Tobiah (2:10). This was a common name in a
powerful family in Ammon, east of Judea.
The name was Jewish, so Tobiah was a Jew by
blood and had been appointed as an official in
Ammon.

13. Summarize what happens in 2:9-12 and what it
reveals about Nehemiah.

_____

_____

_____

14. Summarize what Nehemiah found when he
inspected the walls (see verses 13-15).

_____

_____

_____

By "Jews" (2:16), Nehemiah meant all those who were neither priests, nobles, nor officials. He did not mention the differences among the Jews. Some had accompanied Ezra from Babylon in 458 BC to restore the worship of the Lord according to the Torah. These people would have welcomed the king's change of heart, for they had just tried and failed to rebuild the wall. Still, they already had their own leaders and methods and had never seen Nehemiah before. Other Jews were grandchildren of those who had followed Zerubbabel from Babylon in 538 BC. These had assimilated into the mixed Judean culture; many had pagan wives and mothers, few kept the Law, and most worshipped the Lord alongside other gods. Finally, there were a few Jews (possibly including Tobiah) whose ancestors had never gone into exile. These were perhaps the most assimilated into the surrounding culture.

For Further Study:
Rich insights into Scripture grow from keen observation, which is a learned skill. Reread 2:1-8, and on another sheet of paper, list as many observations as you can about the passage. Try for at least thirty. Sometimes seemingly trivial observations lead to important truths and insights.

These observations should suggest further questions. List at least ten questions (beginning with who, what, when, where, how, or why) that your observations suggest. If you can't answer them now, come back to them after you've worked through more of Nehemiah.

15. In verses 17-18, what reasons did Nehemiah give for trying again to rebuild the wall?

_____

_____

I also told them about the gracious hand of my God on me (2:18). "Nehemiah could personally attest that God was alive and active on his behalf. . . . What was required and what Nehemiah provided was a vision and decisive leadership. Nehemiah was clearly a shaker, a mover, and a doer."[9]

16. How would you characterize the people's response to Nehemiah's invitation, indicated in the last sentence of 2:18?

_____

_____

_____

77

Optional Application: What encourages you to get involved in the "good work" (2:18) of building God's kingdom? How can you discover what your contribution to this work could be?

For Thought and Discussion: Look up Ephesians 6:12.
    a. What can you expect to happen when you begin to follow the Holy Spirit's guidance to do one of His works? Why can you expect this?
    b. Why is it important to see the real powers behind the people obstructing God's work?

Optional Application: What can you learn from 2:19-20 about handling opposition to God's work? Try to apply the principles to a specific situation you are in (whether at work, in your church or a ministry you're involved in, in an evangelism situation, or in serving your family). What action should you take? What action should you *not* take?

"Nehemiah was a man of action and of cooperation. He would explain what needed to be done (2:16-17) and inspire others to join him (2:18)."[10]

17. In 2:19, how did Nehemiah's enemies initially try to discourage him and his followers?

_____

_____

_____

_____

"By his great confidence and dependence on God for success, [Nehemiah] inspired the leaders and the people to a task they had considered beyond their abilities."[11]

"Unlike Assyria in Samaria, Babylon had not imported subjects from across her empire when she took the Jews from Judah in 587 BC. Thus, there was room for the returnees in 538. However, Edomites had moved north from Edom under pressure from immigration from the south and west. Also, the poorest Jews, who had not been exiled, had taken title to all available land. They and some Persian appointees held all the local offices. So the returning exiles had to cultivate land with no clear title to it on sufferance from their neighbors."[12]

18. In 2:20, what significance do you see in Nehemiah's response to his enemies?

_____

_____

_____

_____

Construction Begins

In chapter 3, Nehemiah recorded several names and occupations of those who led the rebuilding of each section of the wall.

19. In Nehemiah 3, notice the descriptions of those who worked side by side in the difficult labor of rebuilding the wall. Besides their names, what other notable information is given about the rebuilders in the following verses?

a. 3:8-12

_____

_____

b. 3:13-16

_____

_____

c. 3:17-21

_____

_____

d. 3:22-27

_____

_____

e. 3:28-32

_____

_____

For Thought and Discussion: Nehemiah had earned the king's trust without sacrificing his allegiance to God. How can Christians seek to do this in our day? (Consider those in authority over us, such as the government or our employer.)

For Further Study: When we receive substantial advice from someone about work we're doing for the Lord, how do we discern whether it is from God? Describe what principles you can discover for this in these passages: Galatians 5:19-23; Philippians 3:18-19; Titus 1:10-11,16; James 3:13-18; 1 John 4:20.

For Thought and Discussion: Nehemiah's enemies failed to discourage him with their threat (see 2:19). They argued that the decision to obey God above all was a rebellion against the state. Do you think this response was wise? Why or why not?

Consider the atti-
tudes displayed by
Nehemiah and the
Jews in 2:9-20. Is
there one you would
like to develop or
strengthen in your
life? If so, jot it down
on a piece of paper;
then write out
the verse that dis-
cusses that attitude.
Memorize and medi-
tate on the verse daily
for the next week,
pray for the attitude,
and look for ways to
practice it.

**For Thought and
Discussion:** What
attitudes that the
builders displayed
in chapter 3 are
worthy examples
for Christians to
adopt when work-
ing together? Which
of their attitudes in
chapter 3 are those
we should avoid?

**Optional
Application:** Can
you think of ways
you could apply any
of the builders' atti-
tudes this week? If so,
describe at least one
first step you could
take to carry this out.

Opposition Intensifies

20. The enemies' first attempt to discourage
    the builders had failed (see 2:19-20). Now,
    in chapter 4, Nehemiah recorded another
    attempt at discouragement. Summarize the
    faults Sanballat and Tobiah found with the
    building project (see 4:2-3).

    _____

    _____

    _____

Will they offer sacrifices? (4:2). This probably
    means something like, "Are these fanatics
    going to pray the wall up? It's their only
    hope!"[13]

21. In responding to this new threat, Nehemiah
    apparently took no action against his oppo-
    nents except in prayer. In 4:4-5, what did he
    ask God to do?

    _____

    _____

In Old Testament context, Nehemiah's prayer
in 4:4-5 was not requesting eternal damna-
tion upon his enemies; rather, he was begging
God not to excuse their conduct but to bring
its consequences upon them in this world. "To
understand such violent language, we need to
appreciate fully the sense of the divine purpose
at work, so that opposition is not seen in human
terms but as opposition to God himself."[14]

22. What progress on the wall is reported in 4:6?

    _____

    _____

The people worked with all their heart (4:6). Literally, "the people had a heart to work."

23. What new threat arises in 4:7-8, and how did Nehemiah respond to it?

_____

_____

_____

We prayed to our God and posted a guard (4:9). "Pray first and commit your cause to God. Pray first and take the steps that seem appropriate. Pray first and let God guide you in what to do in the crisis. Nehemiah understood that principle and practiced it."[15]

24. What fears on the part of the Jews are mentioned in 4:10-12?

_____

_____

25. In the face of these fears, how did Nehemiah encourage the people in verses 13-14?

_____

_____

26. In verse 15, Nehemiah gave two reasons for the plot's failure. What were they?

_____

_____

Don't be afraid. . . . Remember the Lord, who is great and awesome (4:14). "The best way to dispel fear . . . is to remember the Lord who alone is to be feared."[16]

For Thought and Discussion: What do you think of Nehemiah's strong language in his prayer in 4:4-5? Was he failing to love his enemies?

For Thought and Discussion: How can we distinguish helpful from harmful criticism?

For Further Study: Sometimes we need to discern whether to support, question, or withhold judgment on someone else's work. But the Bible urges us not to condemn others' works except in cases of clear sin (see Romans 14:1-4,10-13; 1 Corinthians 4:3-5; Matthew 18:15-17). Consider this dilemma: How do you discern what work to support or question without wrongly judging your brother? (The New Testament verbs translated as *judge* and *discern* are the same word in Greek. See also Luke 9:49-50; 11:23; 1 Corinthians 5:3; Galatians 1:6-9; Philippians 1:9-10; 1 John 4:1.)

Optional Application: In your God-given tasks at this time in your life, how true is it that you have "a heart to work," as the people did in Nehemiah 4:6?

For Thought and Discussion: Look again at 4:14 and 4:20. How does defense based on trust in God differ from defense based on fear? What does it mean for us today to trust God for our defense?

For Further Study: On this topic of fear versus trusting God, describe what you can learn from these passages: Deuteronomy 3:22; 20:3; 31:6; Psalm 33:16-19; Isaiah 31:1; 51:12-13.

Optional Application: Recall how Nehemiah and the builders responded to their fears (see 4:13-23). What fears do you have about laboring for God? What do you think is the best way for you to handle those fears?

27. What further tactics did Nehemiah use in 4:16-23 to keep the people working and maintain progress on the wall?

_____

_____

28. What leadership principles are displayed in Nehemiah's actions at this point?

_____

_____

29. What principles in chapters 1–4 have you discovered that apply particularly to Christian leaders or workers?

_____

_____

_____

30. What would you select as the key verse or passage in Nehemiah 1–4—one that best captures or reflects the dynamics of what these chapters are all about?

_____

_____

31. List any lingering questions you have about Nehemiah 1–4.

_____

_____

_____

For the Group

(In your first meeting on the book of Nehemiah, it may be helpful to turn to the front of this book and review together "For Group Study" on page 7.)

Not everyone is good at outlining and overviews. Those in your group who found these tasks easy might describe how they approached the tasks. There are several ways to divide and outline the book—what process or principles did you follow in choosing the structure that seems best?

Make sure everyone understands how to relate a passage to the overall themes of the whole book. Everyone should come up with a statement of purpose for the book and a list of themes, but you need not all agree on these.

Provide time for members to ask questions about anything they did not understand. For questions that will require additional outside study, you might ask a group member to volunteer to pursue the answers.

Allow time also for members to share how they are applying what they learn in Nehemiah to their own lives.

Finally, remember to set aside time to pray together. Nehemiah faithfully lifted up in prayer his burden for the restoration of Jerusalem. Pray together about specific burdens God might have you bear to Him in prayer. If some needs are already clear to you, begin praying about them as Nehemiah did.

Optional Application: As you review principles and lessons you've discovered in chapters 1–4, do you believe God is leading you to take any action or seek any change in attitude in light of what you've studied and learned? If so, how can you respond?

Specific Prayer Requests

"Praying for particular things," said I, "always seems to me like advising God how to run the world. Wouldn't it be wiser to assume that He knows best?"

"On the same principle," said he, "I suppose you never ask a man next to you to pass the salt, because God knows best whether you ought to have salt or not. And I suppose you never take an umbrella, because God knows best whether you ought to be wet or dry."

"That's quite different," I protested.

"I don't see why," said he. "The odd thing is that He should let us influence the course of events at all. But since He lets us do it in one way I don't see why He shouldn't let us do it in the other."[17]

Discuss any leadings you feel for prayer or for risky action. You might have varying convictions about individual tasks, or several of you might share one. Pray together about these

(continued on page 84)

(continued from page 83)

leadings. Finally, encourage one another to pray and to act on what you hear in prayer.

You may want to discuss any difficulties you're having in taking time for private prayer, listening to God, or accomplishing what you feel led to do. Share especially your fears. How can you "carry each other's burdens" (Galatians 6:2)?

You may want to focus your discussion for lesson 5 especially on the following issues, themes, and concepts. These things will likely reflect what group members have learned in their individual study of this week's passage, although they'll have made discoveries in other areas as well.

- Effective prayer
- The connection between prayer and action
- Nehemiah's character traits
- Principles for effective leadership

The following numbered questions in lesson 5 may stimulate your best and most helpful discussion: 3, 4, 11, 15, 16, 28, 29, 30, and 31.

Look also at the questions in the margin under the heading "For Thought and Discussion."

1. F. Charles Fensham, *The Books of Ezra and Nehemiah* (Grand Rapids, MI: Eerdmans, 1982), 153.
2. Edwin M. Yamauchi, *Ezra-Nehemiah*, in vol. 4 of *The Expositor's Bible Commentary*, ed. Frank E. Gabelein (Grand Rapids, MI: Zondervan, 1990), 685.
3. Yamauchi, 591.
4. Yamauchi, 591.
5. Derek Kidner, *Ezra and Nehemiah: An Introduction and Commentary* (Downers Grove, IL: InterVarsity, 1979), 103.
6. Yamauchi, 591.
7. Yamauchi, 686.
8. W. F. Adeney, "Ezra, Nehemiah, and Esther," in *The Expositor's Bible*, vol. 13, ed. W. R. Nicoll (London: Hodder and Stoughton, n. d.), 196; as cited in Yamauchi, 686–687.
9. Yamauchi, 690.
10. Yamauchi, 591.
11. Yamauchi, 691.
12. Kidner, 8.
13. Kidner, 90.

14. P. R. Ackroyd, *Chronicles, Ezra, Nehemiah* (London: SCM, 1973), 277–278; as cited in Yamauchi, 702.
15. J. I. Packer, *Never Beyond Hope* (Downers Grove, IL: Inter-Varsity, 2000), 169.
16. Yamauchi, 704.
17. C. S. Lewis, *God in the Dock: Essays on Theology and Ethics* (Grand Rapids, MI: Eerdmans, 1970), 217.

NEHEMIAH 5–7

Learning to Overcome

*The wall was completed ... in fifty-two days.
When all our enemies heard about this, all the
surrounding nations were afraid and lost their
self-confidence, because they realized that this
work had been done with the help of our God.*
NEHEMIAH 6:15-16

Read through chapters 5–7 several times, if possible. Then glance through this lesson's subtitles and questions. As you study, keep asking yourself how these chapters reflect Nehemiah's overall themes and purposes.

Love Beyond Law

Read 5:1-19 a few times, noting your observations and questions.

External persecution was not the only threat to the Jews' work; material circumstances and selfishness among the people of God also gave trouble. The people's complaints were:
   1. They could not farm while they built walls, and they could not feed their families on walls (see verse 2).

(continued on page 88)

(continued from page 87)

For Further Study:
To learn more about the practice of "charging your own people interest" (5:7), see Exodus 22:25-26; Leviticus 25:35-37. How did usury differ from lawful lending?

For Further Study:
Study the laws of slavery in Exodus 21:2-11 and Leviticus 25:39-55. What background insight do they provide for Nehemiah's actions in this chapter?

2. Poor harvests (whether because no one was in the fields, because of the enemies' military threat, or because of weather) had forced many people to mortgage their property so that now economic ruin was inevitable (see verse 3).

3. Taxes were aggravating the financial squeeze (see verse 4).

4. Some people's poverty was so extreme that they were even selling some children so they could afford to feed the rest (see verse 5).

5. Worst of all, the men who were buying their children and lending for unpayable mortgages were not strangers at all but fellow Jews (see verses 5 and 7)!

1. In terms of severity, how would you rank the various problems mentioned in 5:1-7?

_____

_____

_____

The law allowed a Jew to sell himself into the service of another, but the buyer had to treat him as a servant hired for a fixed period. The owner had to free his Jewish slave after that period (see Exodus 21:2-11; Leviticus 25:39-55; Deuteronomy 15:12-18).

"Nehemiah was a man of compassion. He renounced his own privileges (5:18) and denounced the wealthy who had exploited their poorer brothers (5:8). He did this because of his reverence for God (5:9,15)."[1]

88

2. In 5:9, what reason did Nehemiah give to the rich for practicing charity rather than strict legality in regard to their Jewish brothers?

_____

_____

3. Think how expensive it was for the rich to support the poor without interest on their loans and without knowing if they would ever get their principal back. Yet Nehemiah condemned anyone who would not do so (see 5:13). Why do you think he spoke so strongly?

_____

_____

4. What do you think about the requirement Nehemiah gave to the rich in 5:11?

_____

_____

5. What was the governor's rightful salary (see 5:14,18)? Beyond that right, what did governors customarily exact from the people (see verse 15)?

_____

_____

_____

6. How did Nehemiah's behavior as governor differ from that of earlier governors (see verses 16-18)?

_____

_____

7. What two reasons did Nehemiah give for his choices (see verses 15 and 18)?

_____

_____

_____

For Thought and Discussion: Do you think 5:1-13 offers any principles for financial interactions between Christians today? Between Christians and non-Christians? In what specific situations would these apply?

For Thought and Discussion: Rebuilding Jerusalem's wall and helping its people were more important to Nehemiah than getting his rightful compensation. He also made his fellow Jews sacrifice their rights. With this in mind, look at 1 Corinthians 9:3-18. What kinds of rights do you think Christians need to sacrifice today in order to work for the building of God's kingdom?

Optional Application: Because of his practices, Nehemiah actually lost money as governor of Judah. Obeying God and serving His people cost him. Might this attitude apply to you in any way? If you think so, explain how.

**Optional
Application:** Has God
called you to sacrifice
any personal rights in
order to live out the
gospel? If so, in what
ways?

**For Thought and
Discussion:** In what
ways do you sense
that Nehemiah expe-
rienced a high degree
of personal fulfill-
ment while carrying
out such demanding
work in the face of
extensive obstacles?

Imagine that during these challenging and difficult times in Judah and Jerusalem—and for
Nehemiah personally—you catch this man in
a rare quiet moment and ask how he is doing.
How would he answer? Was he worn down by
all that was demanded of him? Was his tank
empty or full?

"Nehemiah I think would tell us, if he were
here to testify . . . that zealous, single-
minded service of God doesn't feel like
sacrifice when you're engaged in it. It
feels, rather, like active gratitude, seeking
self-expression in active faithfulness. It
feels, indeed, like living the life that you
were meant to live and that the Lord
redeemed you for.

"Have we, I wonder, all seen this?
Have we started to seek the grace of zeal
for our life with our Lord?"[2]

More Temptations

Read chapter 6 again before continuing.

According to 6:1, the building project at this
time was in its most critical phase. "The open gate-
ways . . . were the enemy's last hope of regaining
the upper hand without actually mounting a siege,
which would be out of the question against fellow
subjects of Persia."[3]

The plain of Ono (6:2). This was apparently neu-
tral territory, halfway between Samaria and
Jerusalem. However, at nineteen miles away it
was more than a day's journey for Nehemiah. It
offered him no protection against attack from
nearby unfriendly districts, and the trip would
have led him away from his post for several
crucial days.

8. Nehemiah said he believed that Sanballat and Geshem were "scheming to harm [him]" (6:2). What do you think their scheme might have been?

_____

_____

9. In 6:5-7, how did Nehemiah's enemies try to frighten him into meeting with them?

_____

_____

10. Why do you think Sanballat sent his message in an "unsealed letter" (6:5)?

_____

_____

_____

11. In 6:5-9, what clues told Nehemiah that the invitation to confer was an attempt to frighten him into abandoning the walls (compare 4:1,7-8)?

_____

_____

_____

12. In 6:9, how did Nehemiah get the courage to continue his work in the face of the threat (compare 1:4-5,8-10)?

_____

_____

_____

I prayed, "Now strengthen my hands" (6:9). "Nehemiah wasn't self-reliant; he was God-reliant. He rejoiced in the faithfulness of God and trusted and prayed. The joy of the Lord and the subjective fruit of his prayer was his strength."[4]

For Thought and Discussion: When receiving a warning from others, how can a Christian distinguish between God-given warnings and those that are mistaken or deceptive?

13. In 6:2-8, what do Nehemiah's responses to these distractions reveal about him? Describe any character traits or principles of leadership you can glean from these incidents.

_____

_____

_____

_____

Shemaiah (6:10). This man may have been a priest.

Shut in (6:10). This may have been because of some ritual uncleanness (see Numbers 19:11-12). It could not have been a serious matter, since he expected soon to enter the temple area.

14. What was Shemaiah's warning in 6:10? What was he trying to convince Nehemiah to do?

_____

_____

_____

15. In 6:11, Nehemiah gave two responses in refusing Shemaiah.

   a. What do his responses reveal about his character?

_____

_____

_____

   b. What do you think Nehemiah's enemies hoped to gain through the false prophecy?

_____

_____

_____

c. What would have happened if Nehemiah had given in to fear?

_____

_____

d. How do you think Nehemiah knew that the warning was not sincere?

_____

_____

Nehemiah "knew how to organize the rebuilding work (chapter 3). . . . He inspired the people with his own example (5:14-18). . . . Remarkably the walls neglected for nearly a century and a half were rebuilt in less than two months when the people were galvanized into action by the catalyst of Nehemiah's leadership."[5]

16. What notable character strengths does Nehemiah reveal in the incident with Shemaiah?

_____

_____

Elul (6:15). August–September, six months after Nehemiah first appealed to the king.

"After fifty-two days of solid slog, the wall was up. This tremendous achievement called for massive organization. . . . It was brilliant. But Nehemiah never ascribed success to his organizational skill; the work was done, he wrote, 'with the help of our God' (6:16)."[6]

For Further Study:
Compare Nehemiah 6:16 to Philippians 1:12-19. Summarize what you feel is a godly response to public slander or persecution.

For Thought and Discussion: Shecaniah, son of Arah (see 6:18), was descended from those who returned to Judea with Zerubbabel (see Ezra 2:5). Tobiah was also connected with the high priest (see Nehemiah 13:4). Thus, professing Jews were undermining Nehemiah's work. How do you think a Christian should respond when people in high places who profess to be servants of God seem to be undermining the work of other servants of God (see Matthew 7:1-5,15-20; 18:15-17; Romans 14:1; 15:1-2)?

For Thought and Discussion: What applicable principles for the Christian life do you discover in 6:15-19?

Fifty-two days (6:15). Probably in the late summer of the year 445 BC.

17. How would you explain the factors that led to the realization on the part of Israel's neighbors mentioned in 6:16?

_____

_____

_____

_____

Under oath (6:18). This was probably contractual. Tobiah was apparently connected with influential Jews by both marriage (to a priestly family; see 13:4) and business.

"Nehemiah was a man who triumphed over opposition. His opponents used every ruse to intimidate him. They started with ridicule (2:19; 4:2-3). They attempted slander (6:5-7). Hired prophets gave him misleading advice (6:10-14). Nehemiah responded with prayer (4:4), with redoubled efforts (4:6), with vigilance (4:9), and with trust in God (4:14)."[7]

The City Put to Use

Read chapter 7, trying not to get bogged down in details; instead, look for the overall purpose of the chapter. Also, be alert for themes and development that you find most important as well as questions that come to your mind.

Imagine Nehemiah's feelings at this point in time, after all he'd been through—"the wall had been rebuilt and I had set the doors in place" (7:1). Yet there was still much to do.

The gatekeepers, the musicians and the Levites
(7:1). Some gatekeepers guarded the city gates; others guarded the holy place and its valuables. The musicians performed the music and choral prayers for temple worship. The Levites each had assigned tasks for temple upkeep.

For Further Study: Why do you think Nehemiah wanted to know the ancestry of everyone who claimed to be a Jew? Why was the connection to Israel before the exile so important in solving the problem of repopulating Jerusalem (see 2:20; see also Genesis 17:8)?

18. The building project was not an end in itself but a means to something further. What does the appointment of gatekeepers, musicians, and Levites (see 7:1) tell you about the purpose of the city?

_____

_____

_____

19. Does the purpose of the holy city suggest anything about God's purposes for His holy people today (compare Ephesians 1:5-6; 1 Peter 2:9)?

_____

_____

20. According to 7:5-7, what was the record that Nehemiah copied into verses 6-72?

_____

_____

The temple servants (7:46); *descendants of the servants of Solomon* (7:57). David created a corps of assistants to the Levites to take some of the more menial tasks of temple upkeep. Solomon evidently added a further group of assistants. Some of these men seem to have been descended from converts to the worship of the Lord in David's day, as the list includes non-Hebrew names (they are family names, not first names). At least at that time, purity of ancestry had been less important than a sincere commitment to God's commands, including circumcision.

Optional Application:
According to some views of this book's structure and purpose, everything that has happened so far in Nehemiah is building toward the revival of faith and godliness in Judah that is shown in chapters 8–9. Do the events in Nehemiah's book suggest any ways that the church today might cooperate with God in reviving faith and obedience? If so, how can you participate in this, in cooperation with God?

Optional Application: Review the principles and lessons you've discovered in chapters 5–7. Do you believe that God is leading you to take any action or seek any change in attitude in light of what you've studied and learned? If so, how can you respond?

Urim and Thummim (7:65). See Ezra 2:63; Exodus 28:30; Numbers 27:21; Deuteronomy 33:8; 1 Samuel 14:41; 28:6.

_____

21. What does 7:5-73 indicate about God's view of family?

_____

_____

_____

_____

The seventh month (7:73). The month immediately after the wall was finished. The first day of the month was the Festival of Trumpets (later known as Rosh Hashanah). Today this festival marks the beginning of a new civil year, while the religious year changes at Passover. For more on the Festival of Trumpets, see Leviticus 23:23-25; Numbers 29:1-6.

In their own towns (7:73). Few people lived in Jerusalem (see 7:4,73); most lived in distant villages. However, it was required that all Jews assemble in Jerusalem on the Festival of Trumpets.

_____

22. What would you select as the key verse or passage in Nehemiah 5–7—one that best captures or reflects the dynamics of what these chapters are all about?

_____

_____

23. List any lingering questions you have about Nehemiah 5–7.

_____

_____

_____

_____

96

For the Group

Be prepared to clarify the Old Testament laws of
lending and slavery that form the background
for Nehemiah 5. (A Bible dictionary or handbook
can be useful for this, as well as Old Testament
commentaries.) Once you all understand what the
law stated, discuss the moral values behind it, and
how those unchanging values apply to Christians.
Then see how your lives in particular might
better reflect the attitudes that Nehemiah was
promoting.

How can you help one another to resist tempta-
tions like those Nehemiah faced in these chapters?
How can you help one another to discern whether
counsel is from God or the enemy? How can you
help one another to acquire the commendable character qualities shown by Nehemiah and others in
these chapters?

Continue to share together the principles
you've found and how you're applying them to
your lives. Keep encouraging each other to persevere with past applications. Discuss any specific
dilemmas that group members may be facing in
their lives as they seek to be obedient to God's
Word.

You may want to focus your discussion for
lesson 6 especially on the following issues, themes,
and concepts. These will likely reflect what group
members have learned in their individual study of
this week's passage, although they'll have made
discoveries in other areas as well.

- Justice and compassion for the needy
- Overcoming opposition
- Effective leadership in challenging
  circumstances
- Effective prayer
- The connection between prayer and action
- Nehemiah's character traits
- Diligent, wholehearted work

The following numbered questions in lesson 6
may stimulate your best and most helpful discussion: 1, 15, 16, 17, 19, 21, 22, and 23.

Look also at the questions in the margin under
the heading "For Thought and Discussion."

1. Edwin M. Yamauchi, *Ezra-Nehemiah,* in vol. 4 of *The Expositor's Bible Commentary,* ed. Frank E. Gabelein (Grand Rapids, MI: Zondervan, 1990), 591.
2. J. I. Packer, *Never Beyond Hope* (Downers Grove, IL: Inter-Varsity, 2000), 170–171.
3. Derek Kidner, *Ezra and Nehemiah: An Introduction and Commentary* (Downers Grove, IL: InterVarsity, 1979), 98.
4. Packer, 169.
5. Yamauchi, 591, 715.
6. Packer, 167–168.
7. Yamauchi, 591.

NEHEMIAH 8–10

A Spiritual Revival

This day is holy to our Lord. Do not grieve, for the joy of the LORD is your strength.

NEHEMIAH 8:10

Read Nehemiah 8–10 several times and recall the context of where the story is moving. Do you have a sense of how these chapters fit the book's themes?

Revival

1. What event was planned for the festival assembly (see 8:1)? Who requested this event, and who attended?

_____

_____

_____

_____

Assembly (8:2). In the Septuagint (the Greek Old Testament used by Jews of Jesus' day), the Hebrew word for "assembly" was translated *ekklesia*. Paul frequently used this word in his letters, where it is translated into English as "church."

For Thought and Discussion: To what extent could the public reading of Scripture in Nehemiah 8:1-8 be an example and model for Christian gatherings today?

2. Notice the behavior of the people in 8:3-6. What do you think motivated their response? Do you think their attitude toward God's Word was a necessary first step toward a revival of allegiance to God? Why or why not?

_____

_____

_____

_____

Levites (8:7). These men apparently moved through the crowd, while the men named in 8:4 remained on the platform to assist with the reading.

Making it clear (8:8). The people may have understood the Hebrew being read aloud but needed explanation, which the teachers provided section by section as the reading proceeded. Or the teachers may have been translating the reading if the hearers knew only the Aramaic language.

Nehemiah the governor, Ezra the priest and teacher of the Law (8:9). "Nehemiah, a layman, was able to cooperate with his contemporary Ezra, the scribe and priest, in spite of the fact that these two leaders were of entirely different temperaments. In reaction to the problem of mixed marriages, Ezra plucked out his own hair (Ezra 9:3), whereas Nehemiah plucked out the hair of the offenders (Nehemiah 13:25)!"[1]

3. In the last sentence of 8:9, why do you think the people responded as they did to what they heard from the Law?

_____

_____

_____

4. What did Nehemiah tell the people to do instead of their first reaction (see 8:9-10)? What reasons did he give?

_____

_____

_____

Do not grieve (8:10). "The powerful exposition of the Word of God can bring deep conviction of sin. But repentance must not degenerate into a self-centered remorse but must issue into joy in God's forgiving goodness (cf. 2 Corinthians 2:5-11)."[2]

---

5. Nehemiah announced to the people in 8:10, "This day is holy [sacred] to our Lord."

   a. Why do you think Nehemiah declared it a holy day?

   _____

   _____

   b. What were the reasons for the holiness of this occasion?

   _____

   _____

   c. What do you think the day's holiness had to do with the tension of celebration versus mourning?

   _____

   _____

6. Nehemiah told the people to share their feasts with the less fortunate—with "those who have nothing prepared" (8:10). What attitudes were demonstrated by this sharing?

   _____

   _____

For Further Study:
Compare the kind of sharing Nehemiah commanded in 8:10 with the social consciousness and concern reflected in these passages: Exodus 23:11; Leviticus 19:10; 23:22; Deuteronomy 14:28-29; 26:12-13; Job 29:12,16; 31:16-19; Psalm 112:9; Proverbs 1:6-8; 2:2. What do these passages together indicate about God's concern for the needy?

Optional Application: In your own life, in what way does the reading of God's Word bring to you a true and proper joy—the joy of the Lord, which is your strength?

For Thought and Discussion: What particular elements of spiritual revival do you see mentioned in 8:1-12?

Optional Application: Can you think of any step of action you might take to encourage or sustain a revival in your own devotion to God? If so, describe that action.

_____

_____

7. How would you define and explain "the joy of the LORD" (8:10)? Why is it our strength?

_____

_____

_____

Able to understand (8:2) . . . *men, women and others who could understand* (8:3) . . . *so that the people understood* (8:8) . . . *they now understood* (8:12). This understanding describes a thorough grasp of the reading's meaning. It goes beyond just knowing what the text says.

---

8. Why do you think the kind of "understanding" mentioned in 8:2,3,8,12 was so important to the revival?

_____

_____

9. Why do you think the people responded first in grief and then in joy once they had heard and understood God's Word? How might this progression relate to people's responses to the gospel today?

_____

_____

_____

10. On the day after the events of 8:1-12, some of the people met with Ezra "to give attention to the words of the Law" (verse 13). Who

were those people, and what did their actions indicate about their appetite for God's Word?

_____

_____

_____

_____

Live in temporary shelters during the festival of the seventh month (8:14). See Leviticus 23:33-43; Numbers 29:12-30; Deuteronomy 16:13-17.

11. Describe how the Jews celebrated the Festival of Tabernacles in 8:15-18.

_____

_____

_____

> The Festival of Tabernacles, or Booths, lasted for eight days, beginning on the fifteenth day of the seventh month. The tabernacles were tents like those in which the Israelites lived while they wandered with Moses. The tabernacles were meant to remind the Jews of their ancestors' miraculous deliverance from slavery and of God's care for them in the desert as they journeyed from Egypt to the Promised Land.

From the days of Joshua son of Nun until that day (8:17). "Never since the time of Joshua (Jeshua) was such a feast celebrated. What is the meaning of this? . . . It might refer to the spirit in which it was celebrated. For the first time since Joshua this feast was held in the same spirit as that of ancient times."[3]

Day after day . . . Ezra read from the Book of the Law of God (8:18). "On every day of the

Optional Application: Is there anything you could do to encourage spiritual revival in your church and community? How might you accomplish this goal?

For Further Study: Learn more about the Festival of Tabernacles in Leviticus 23:39; see also Exodus 23:16 and 34:22, where the Festival of Tabernacles is called the Festival of Ingathering.

103

In the Festival of
Tabernacles, as they
remembered and cel-
ebrated their people's
deliverance from
bondage in Egypt,
how could the Jews'
attitudes enrich the
way we celebrate our
salvation at Easter?

**Optional
Application:** Pray for
ways to begin living
the truths you see in
8:10-12. How might a
group of Christians (in
a Bible study group
or a church) help each
other celebrate holi-
ness and God's Word
with joy?

seven days of the festival Ezra read from the
Pentateuch, as prescribed in Deuteronomy 31:11.
It shows that Ezra had followed precisely the
precepts of Deuteronomy and also of Leviticus."[4]

Confession

The last day of the Festival of Tabernacles was the
twenty-second of the month. Two days later they
assembled, as 9:1 describes.

12. Why do you think the assembled Jews were
    fasting, were wearing sackcloth, and putting
    dust on their heads (see 9:1), after they'd earlier
    been encouraged toward joy in 8:10?

    _____

    _____

"The . . . problem, namely, that we have
a sudden change from joy to confession
of sins, can be solved if we keep in mind
that the Israelites were already weeping
and mourning on the first of the month
after they had heard the law. The Levites
requested that they celebrate a feast of
joy, but after this feast it would be natural
for them to think again of their sins and
iniquities. These sins were not yet atoned
for. . . . The best solution is to regard this
assembly as something unique which
happened on that occasion under
special circumstances."[5]

Separated themselves from all foreigners (9:2).
This does not necessarily mean they divorced
and broke social relations with everyone who
lacked pure Jewish blood. (See also 10:30 and
13:3.)

13. "A fourth of the day" (9:3, NASB) was about three hours. What two things did the Jews do on this day for three hours each (see verses 2-3)?

_____

_____

Cried out (9:4). The word implies sorrow.

14. The sorrowful cry (see verse 4) led into a prayer that included worship (see verses 5-8) and confession (see verses 33-35). How would you explain the basic relationship between worship and confession and between praise and sorrow?

_____

_____

_____

15. Use the following chart to record what each section of the prayer in Nehemiah 9 has to say about God's acts and His character.

	GOD'S ACTS	GOD'S CHARACTER
9:5-6		
9:7-8		
9:9-12		
9:13-15		
9:16-18		
9:19-21		
9:22-25		
9:26-31		
9:32-37		

For Further Study: An interesting observation: "The ninth chapters of Ezra, Nehemiah and Daniel are devoted to confessions of national sin and to prayers for God's grace."[6] How would you compare the circumstances and content of the prayers in Ezra 9:5-15, Nehemiah 9:5-37, and Daniel 9:3-19?

For Further Study:
In 9:29, notice the acknowledgment that a person will "live" if he obeys God's commandments. Should this statement be taken literally? Why or why not? What kind of life is referred to here? In forming your answers, look also at these Scriptures and their contexts: Leviticus 18:5; Deuteronomy 30:16; Ezekiel 20:11,13,21; Luke 10:28; Romans 10:5; Galatians 3:12.

For Thought and Discussion: In the prayer in 9:5-37, what principles can you find for how God's people should confess their sins?

For Further Study:
Compare the content and structure of the prayer in 9:5-37 with Psalm 106. What are the significant similarities, and what are the significant differences?

For Thought and Discussion: Explain how chapter 9 witnesses to both the justice and the mercy of God.

16. According to the words of the prayer in 9:5-31, what are the highlights of Israel's national history in the consciousness of the Jews at this time?

_____

_____

_____

*You are the L*ORD *God, who chose Abram* (9:7).
"In the Old Testament, the choice is always the action of God, of his grace, and always contains a mission for man; and only out of this mission can man comprehend the choice of God. . . . Thus, when Nehemiah 9:7 says that Yahweh has already chosen Abraham, this fits the situation of the prayer in this context, the purpose of which was to make known in the syncretism of the time of Ezra and Nehemiah that Judah has the mission of maintaining her identity and of resisting the temptation to be assimilated by the nations, as long as election is to mean a mission to the nations."[7]

17. How did God respond to Israel's disobedience in 9:18-21, and how does this response reflect His compassion?

_____

_____

_____

18. Study the sequence of events mentioned in 9:25-31. From those events, what can you discover . . .

about human nature?

_____

_____

_____

about God?

_____

_____

_____

19. How did God respond to Israel's disobedience in 9:26-27—and again, how did this reflect His compassion?

_____

_____

_____

20. What is the significance of what the people acknowledged about God in 9:32?

_____

_____

21. What was the people's perspective on how God had treated them, as stated in 9:33?

_____

_____

22. In 9:33-37, what did the Jews see as the cause of their misfortune?

_____

_____

23. How did these Jews understand God's grace, as evidenced, for example, in verses 7-8, 17, 20, and 31-32 of chapter 9?

_____

_____

Recommitment

As you focus on the "binding agreement" of 9:38 that continues through chapter 10, don't get bogged

Optional Application: Which of the qualities of God that you observed in Nehemiah 9 do you find most encouraging as you face the demands of life, and why?

Optional Application: Are there any lessons about prayer in chapter 9 that you might apply to your own prayer life? If so, what are they?

The
Jews in this prayer
spoke of themselves
as those "who sepa-
rated themselves
from the neighboring
peoples for the sake
of the Law of God"
(10:28). Why was this
kind of separation so
important for them,
especially from God's
perspective?

For Further Study:
The separation from
foreign peoples
that is in focus
in Nehemiah 10
reflects a strong Old
Testament theme. List
what reasons for this
kind of separation
are indicated in the
following passages:
Exodus 34:12-16;
Leviticus 20:26;
1 Kings 11:1-4.

For Further Study:
With Nehemiah 10
in mind, look at
2 Corinthians 6:14–7:1.
Why did Paul com-
mand Christians not
to marry pagans?

down in the names (see 10:2-27), but do observe
details from the rest of the passage. Keep the book's
themes in mind.

We are making a binding agreement (9:38). This
   agreement is spelled out in chapter 10. The
   signers of the agreement are listed first (see
   10:1-27), and then the terms of the agreement
   (see verses 28-39).

---

24. In 9:38 we read that the agreement was made
    because of the confession and prayer of 9:5-37.
    Why do you think it was crucial that this agree-
    ment followed that prayer?

    _____

    _____

25. Nehemiah 10:1-27 is a legal listing of the names
    of the leading signatories to the binding agree-
    ment. Nehemiah's name heads the list. What
    other names here do you see repeated from the
    list in chapter 3 of those who rebuilt the wall?

    _____

    _____

    _____

    _____

    _____

"The long list of those who put their
names to the covenant is designed
to show that the entire community—
priests, Levites, and lay leaders—was
wholeheartedly behind it. These are
prominent people in the community;
many of their names have appeared
before in Nehemiah."[8]

26. How does 10:28 summarize the human parties who were concurring to this agreement?

_____

_____

_____

27. List what all these people agreed to do, or not do, according to the following verses:

a. 10:29

_____

_____

b. 10:30

_____

_____

c. 10:31

_____

_____

d. 10:32-33

_____

_____

e. 10:34

_____

_____

f. 10:35-37

_____

_____

g. 10:38

_____

_____

For Further Study: Christ ate and stayed with immoral Jews and pagans. So did His apostles. What do you think holiness (separation) means today for Christians who have been commissioned to bring the gospel to unbelievers? Think of as many principles as you can (see Matthew 15:10-11; 17-20; Luke 5:27-32; 10:30-37; 14:12-14; 1 Corinthians 5:9-13; Ephesians 5:11).

For Further Study: The Law forbade Jews from working or causing anyone to work on the Sabbath, and such work included buying anything from pagans. Read Exodus 20:8-11 and Deuteronomy 5:12-15. Why were the Jews supposed to keep the Sabbath holy?

For Thought and Discussion: In what ways does the practice of the Sabbath offer appropriate principles for a Christian lifestyle? Support your answer with Scripture references as much as possible.

_____

_____

Forgo working the land (10:31). According to Exodus 23:10-11, there was to be a year of rest from farming, similar to there being a day of rest in the week. The reason given was so that poor people and wild animals could take whatever they wanted from the fallow fields. The Jews' mayor may not have known that leaving a field fallow for a year keeps it more fertile by allowing nutrients in the soil to replenish themselves.

Cancel all debts (10:31). In the sabbatical year, everyone who had loaned money to another Jew was to release him from that debt.

This release meant at least that nothing was due during that seventh year. It may also have meant that the debt was permanently canceled or at least the repayment postponed, as cancellation would have upset people's legitimate property rights (see also Deuteronomy 15:1-3).

For Thought and Discussion: Do you think the values, attitudes, and practices of the Sabbath year offer any principles for Christians today? Why or why not? In what ways would observance of the Sabbath year require a person's trust in God?

For Further Study: Read Leviticus 25:4-7,20-22. How did God promise to provide food when no one planted?

For Thought and Discussion: Do you think the law of suspending or canceling debts teaches any values, attitudes, or practices for Christians today? If so, what? If not, why not?

Optional Application: Does your study of the Jews' covenant agreement in Nehemiah 10 suggest any action you might take in your life? If so, what might it be?

28. What attitudes toward worship are reflected in the details of the agreement given in 10:32-39?

_____

_____

_____

29. What would you select as the key verse or passage in Nehemiah 8–10—one that best captures or reflects the dynamics of what these chapters are all about?

_____

_____

_____

30. List any lingering questions you have about Nehemiah 8–10.

_____

_____

_____

For the Group

Ask if anyone would like to share with the group at least one personal application from your previous lessons. You might also discuss how your private and group prayer has affected your attitudes and decisions over the last few weeks.

Be prepared to study the Old Testament laws that form the background for many aspects of the agreement made by the people in chapter 10.

You may want to focus your discussion for lesson 7 especially on the following issues, themes, and concepts. These will likely reflect what group members have learned in their individual study of this week's passage, although they'll have made discoveries in other areas as well.

- The crucial importance of God's Word
- The right environment for spiritual revival
- Confession and repentance
- Effective worship and celebration
- Obedience
- Commitment
- Grief over our sins, joy for our salvation

The following numbered questions in lesson 7 may stimulate your best and most helpful discussion: 2, 7, 8, 14, 18, 20, 29, and 30.

Remember to look also at the "Thought and Discussion" questions in the margin.

1. Edwin M. Yamauchi, _Ezra-Nehemiah_, in vol. 4 of _The Expositor's Bible Commentary_, ed. Frank E. Gabelein (Grand Rapids, MI: Zondervan, 1990), 591.
2. Yamauchi, 725.
3. F. Charles Fensham, _The Books of Ezra and Nehemiah_ (Grand Rapids, MI: Eerdmans, 1982), 221.
4. Fensham, 221.
5. Fensham, 222–223.

6. *NIV Study Bible* (Grand Rapids, MI: Zondervan, 1985), on Nehemiah 9:1-37.
7. T. Vriezen and H. Seebass, *Theological Wordbook of the Old Testament*, 2:87; further cited in Yamauchi, 732.
8. *ESV Study Bible* (Wheaton, IL: Crossway, 2008), on Nehemiah 10:1-27.

NEHEMIAH 11–13
Faithful to the Finish

On that day they offered great sacrifices, rejoicing because God had given them great joy. The women and children also rejoiced. The sound of rejoicing in Jerusalem could be heard far away.
NEHEMIAH 12:43

Read chapters 11–13 before you begin to study. You can skim the lists of names in chapters 11 and 12, but notice the categories of people listed. Think about what all this has to do with the point of the story.

The Holy City

1. Recall from 7:4 that few people lived in Jerusalem. In light of that, what is significant about the information given in chapter 11?

   _____

   _____

2. What significance do you see in the listing of the priests and Levites in verses 1-26 of chapter 12?

   _____

   _____

For Further Study:
12:1-26 lists the high priests, priestly divisions, and Levites from the first return of exiles in 538 BC until Nehemiah's time. Why do you think the family continuity of priests and Levites over a century was important enough to include (see Numbers 3:9-13, especially verse 10)?

Beginning in 12:27, for the first time since 7:5, we return to Nehemiah's first-person voice. This continues for the rest of the book.

The dedication of the wall (12:27). This dedication probably occurred shortly after the events of chapters 8–10.

3. What was to be the chief way of celebrating the wall's dedication (see 12:27)?

_____

_____

_____

4. The priests and Levites prepared for the celebration by purifying themselves, the people, the gates, and the wall (see 12:30). This was probably ceremonial washing. Why do you think everyone and everything needed to be washed (see Leviticus 11:44-45; Numbers 8:21)?

_____

_____

_____

Choirs (12:31,40). This word translates a single Hebrew word meaning "thanksgivings" or "confessions."

"The two great processions probably started from the area of the Valley Gate (2:13,15; 3:13) near the center of the western section of the wall. The first procession, led by Ezra (verse 36), moved in a counterclockwise direction upon the wall; the second, with Nehemiah (verse 38), moved in a clockwise direction. Both met between the Water Gate (verse 37) and the Gate of the Guard (verse 39), then entered the temple area."[1]

5. In celebration of the wall's dedication, what form of pageantry was followed in 12:31-43?

_____

_____

6. Summarize how the Jews celebrated (see 12:27,35,42-43).

_____

_____

_____

"The dedication of the wall culminates the efforts of the people under Nehemiah's inspired leadership. Great enthusiasm must have characterized their march to the joyful music."[2]

7. Compare the procession and celebration of the wall to Psalm 48:11-14. Besides thanking God for what He had done and praising Him for who He is, what were other purposes of such a procession?

_____

_____

_____

This celebration was a very special occasion; ordinary worship would not have been so elaborate. Nevertheless, the account gives a sense of how Jews liked to worship their God.

After the dedication, the Jews were evidently all enthusiastic about supporting Jerusalem worship (see 12:44-47). Even people who were not wealthy had to pay for professional musicians, priests, and temple workers. The priests and Levites were the nation's only civil service and performed many duties; nevertheless, much of the money supported worship services.

For Thought and Discussion: Does 12:30 suggest to you any principles for a Christian's life or worship? Name those principles, or explain why you think the verse is no longer relevant.

For Thought and Discussion: Do you learn anything about worship or celebration from 12:27-47 that could enrich Christian practices? If so, what ideas do you get?

For Thought and Discussion: Do you think Judah's effort and expense for worship offer any principles for Christians? (For instance, would such expense be acceptable today?) Why or why not?

8. Why do you think all this effort and expense for worship (see 12:44-47) was important to the Jews?

_____

_____

_____

_____

9. What situation was discovered in 13:1-3, and how did the Jews respond to it?

_____

_____

_____

_____

There it was found written (13:1). In Deuteronomy 23:3-6.

Curse (13:2). "Curses had a dynamic power of their own once uttered and could not simply be recalled. They could, however, be canceled by blessings (cf. Judges 17:1-2)."[3]

Final Reforms

Recall that shortly after the dedication of the wall, in his first year as governor, Nehemiah had seen to it that honest men were put in charge of the valuable temple furnishings and the stores that supported the temple worship (see 12:44). Eliashib, as high priest, had been made the top man in charge. For twelve years, while Nehemiah had been governor, everything had apparently been done honestly. Then, in about 433 BC, Nehemiah had returned to Persia (see 13:6), and during his absence from Judea, some of the zeal of the Jews' spiritual revival had cooled and abuses had crept in.

After some unspecified time, he had been reappointed governor of Judah (see 13:6-7).

116

"Chapter 13 is the end of his personal memoirs. In it Nehemiah tells us what he found when he came back to Jerusalem as governor several years after his first spell had finished and what he did about it.

"What Nehemiah found was a great deal that, by God's grace, he had set in order during his first term as governor had gone awry and now had to be put back into shape. This was immensely disappointing for him, although he is so tight-lipped about his feelings that the less-than-thoughtful reader can miss the hints of how acutely distressed he became when he discovered how much had gone wrong. The hints are there, however, in the violence of his restorative actions. . . . He's prepared to do anything within reason to get temple worship back on its feet, to get family life back in shape and to get the Sabbath reverently observed in Jerusalem."[4]

10. Summarize the problem identified in 13:4-5.

_____

_____

_____

_____

_____

Closely associated with (13:4). This may indicate a family connection between Eliashib and Tobiah.

For Thought and Discussion: How are Nehemiah's actions in 13:8 similar to the way Jesus responded in Matthew 21:12-13?

11. Why do you think Tobiah wanted to live in a temple storeroom? (Think about what a base in the temple situated him to do.)

_____

_____

12. Explain why Eliashib's act mentioned in 13:7 was sinful.

_____

_____

13. What do you learn about Nehemiah from his response as indicated in 13:8-9? Why do you think the Jews had not already taken this same action before Nehemiah returned?

_____

_____

_____

"Nehemiah was a man of a volcanic temperament who quickly expressed his indignation by taking action."[5]

"If on his first visit he had been a whirlwind, on his second he was all fire and earthquake to a city that had settled down in his absence to a comfortable compromise with the gentile world."[6]

14. What principles for biblical leadership do you see in Nehemiah's example in 13:4-9?

_____

_____

_____

_____

15. What sign of decay does Nehemiah discover in 13:10? What attitudes toward worship and financial priorities does this change in behavior suggest?

_____

_____

_____

For Further Study:
Tithes are mentioned in Nehemiah 13:12 (see also 12:44). Do you think the principle of tithing applies to Christians? If so, how and why? If not, why not (see Matthew 23:23; 1 Corinthians 9:7,14; Philippians 4:15-19)?

16. What further principles of leadership or obedience do you learn from Nehemiah's response in 13:11-13?

_____

_____

_____

17. How do Nehemiah's actions in 13:13 compare with the actions taken by the apostles in the New Testament church in Acts 6:1-5?

_____

_____

_____

18. Summarize what Nehemiah discovered in 13:15-16.

_____

_____

_____

19. Review the Jews' attitude toward the Sabbath as indicated by their agreement in 10:31, and then describe the changes in their attitudes as indicated in 13:15-16.

_____

_____

_____

For Further Study:
Nehemiah feared
that God would
punish the sin of
Sabbath-breaking
(see 13:15-16) as
He had punished it
before (verse 18). He
was thinking of the
words of Jeremiah,
who prophesied to
Judah just before
Babylon crushed her.
Read Jeremiah 17:19-
27. Why do you think
Sabbath-breaking
was so serious?

**For Thought and
Discussion:** How
do you decide what
relevance, if any, Old
Testament commands
such as keeping a
holy place, tithing,
the Sabbath, and
notions of ownership
and sharing have for
modern Christians?

**For Thought and
Discussion:** Observe
how Nehemiah
treated the men who
had taken foreign
wives (see 13:25). Why
do you suppose he
reacted like this?

**For Thought and
Discussion:** Why do
you think the Jews
found it so hard to
keep from allying
themselves with
unbelievers?

20. In 13:17-22, observe Nehemiah's response and
the measures he took to put an end to this
abuse. What strong traits of a leader or principles
of leadership can you find in this response?

_____

_____

_____

21. In 13:23-30, we see yet another lapse among
the Jews that Nehemiah discovered. During his
absence, they had intermarried with the very
pagans from whom they had three times promised to separate (see 9:2; 10:30; 13:3). What
effect on the children of those mixed marriages
particularly dismayed Nehemiah, and why?
(See 13:24,26.)

_____

_____

_____

22. The Jews had sworn to avoid each of the sins
into which they fell while Nehemiah was away
(see 10:28-39). Some (chiefly intermarriage)
were sins they struggled with repeatedly. When
they rededicated themselves yet again during
Nehemiah's second term as governor, what
response do you think they expected from God?
Please explain.

_____

_____

_____

23. What principles for the Christian life can you
discover in the record of Nehemiah's final
reforms in 13:23-31?

_____

_____

_____

_____

What I have so faithfully done (13:14). Literally, "acts of covenant love."

24. Three times in chapter 13, Nehemiah asked God to remember him and his deeds (see also 5:19). For what did he say he wanted to be remembered (see 13:14,22,31)?

_____

_____

25. In 13:29, for what did Nehemiah ask God to remember the corrupt priests (see also 4:4-5; 6:14)?

_____

_____

"Nehemiah was a man with right motivation. Although he justified his ministry, his primary motive was not to be judged aright by others or to be remembered by posterity. The last words of Nehemiah—'Remember me with favor, O my God' (13:31)—recapitulate a frequently repeated theme (5:19; 13:14,22,29). His motive throughout his ministry was to please and serve his divine Sovereign. His only reward would be God's approbation."[7]

26. What would you select as the key verse or passage in Nehemiah 11–13—one that best captures or reflects the dynamics of what these chapters are all about?

_____

_____

_____

For Thought and Discussion: What do you think about Nehemiah's prayers to be remembered for his deeds? Did he believe he'd been earning God's favor?

For Further Study: In what ways was Nehemiah's life and ministry a fulfillment of the prophecies in Isaiah 58:12 and 61:4? In what ways are those prophecies not yet fulfilled?

Optional Application: You may have committed yourself to some actions during your study of Nehemiah. Are you satisfied with your follow-through on these commitments? If not, review the reasons why you made those commitments. If they still hold up, pray about how you can live obediently in response to what God asks of you.

Optional Application: Has your prayer life grown since you began this study? If so, what has been the most significant factor in this growth?

27. List any lingering questions you have about Nehemiah 11–13.

_____

_____

_____

_____

Reviewing Nehemiah

Your review of Nehemiah will be most fruitful if you once more reread the whole book. That may sound like a lot of work, but you'll find that the results will go a long way in helping you retain a thorough grasp of Nehemiah. Look again for themes, the story's movement, actions of major characters, and clues to the author's purpose.

28. How would you summarize what has happened to God's people over the course of time covered by the books of Ezra and Nehemiah?

_____

_____

_____

_____

_____

_____

_____

29. Considering that all of Scripture testifies ultimately of Christ, where does Jesus come most in focus for you in this book?

_____

_____

_____

_____

"The two centuries of the Persian empire were among the most formative periods of Jewish history. Out of the ruins of the little kingdom of Judah there had emerged the small community whose concern to be the people of God by pedigree and practice shaped it into the nation which meets us in the New Testament. Already the future prominence of the Temple and its priests, of the law and its scribes, as well as the enmity between Jews and Samaritans, could be seen developing."[8]

30. What have you especially learned in Nehemiah about the following topics?

a. God's plan in history

_____

_____

b. God's character

_____

_____

c. prayer

_____

_____

d. obedience

_____

_____

e. leadership

_____

_____

Optional Application: Have you made any discoveries in Nehemiah that you feel will help you become more sensitive to God's work in your life, more able to respond to Him in practical obedience? If so, write down what this has meant for you.

Optional Application: Which verses in Nehemiah would be most helpful for you to memorize so you have them always available in your mind and heart for the Holy Spirit to use?

f. building God's kingdom

_____

_____

For the Group

There is much in this lesson that can spark fruitful discussions.

You may want to focus your discussion on just one of the abuses Nehemiah discovered on his return to Jerusalem (see chapter 13), exploring what it implied at the time and what principles for Christians it suggests. Examine Nehemiah's character as well.

By God's grace, you should finish your study with a grasp of the themes of Nehemiah, a sense of how you have grown individually and corporately, and a direction for further study and growth.

You may want to focus your discussion for lesson 8 especially on the following issues, themes, and concepts. These will likely reflect what group members have learned in their individual study of this week's passage, although they'll have made discoveries in other areas as well.

* Holiness, purity, and separation
* Effective prayer
* The connection between prayer and action
* Nehemiah's character traits
* Principles for effective leadership

The following numbered questions in lesson 8 may stimulate your best and most helpful discussion: 13, 14, 15, 16, 20, 23, 26, and 27.

Once more, look also at the questions in the margin under the heading "For Thought and Discussion."

Allow enough discussion time to look back together and review the book of Nehemiah as a whole. You can use the numbered questions 28, 29, and 30 in this lesson to help you do that. As you discuss these, evaluate how the group functioned during your study. What would you do the same or differently?

Also, identify members' current needs and decide what you might want to study together next.

1. *NIV Study Bible* (Grand Rapids, MI: Zondervan, 1985), on Nehemiah 12:31.
2. Edwin M. Yamauchi, *Ezra-Nehemiah*, in vol. 4 of *The Expositor's Bible Commentary*, ed. Frank E. Gabelein (Grand Rapids, MI: Zondervan, 1990), 756.
3. Yamauchi, 759.
4. J. I. Packer, *Never Beyond Hope* (Downers Grove, IL: InterVarsity, 2000), 159–160, 162.
5. Yamauchi, 761.
6. Derek Kidner, *Ezra and Nehemiah: An Introduction and Commentary* (Downers Grove, IL: InterVarsity, 1979), 129.
7. Yamauchi, 591.
8. Kidner, 17.

GOING ON IN EZRA AND NEHEMIAH

Now that you've completed this study guide, you might feel you haven't yet finished with the books of Ezra and Nehemiah. Perhaps you want to return to matters that you explored only briefly during your study. Here are some suggested ways to pursue further study of the books of Ezra and Nehemiah or to take a closer look in the rest of the Old Testament at some of the issues the books raise.

1. Recall again how Ezra committed himself to studying God's Word, doing it, and teaching it. Look in the following passages to explore more dynamics related to living a life that stays true to the Word of God in every aspect: Psalm 119; Ecclesiastes 12:11; Isaiah 55:10-11; Jeremiah 23:29; Malachi 2:7; Matthew 5:19; 7:24; John 8:31-32; 13:17; Romans 1:16; Acts 4:31; 2 Corinthians 2:17; 4:2; 10:4-5; Ephesians 6:17; Colossians 1:25; 2 Timothy 3:16-17; 4:2; Titus 2:1; Hebrews 4:12; 1 Peter 1:23.

2. Recall how Nehemiah saw himself as standing "in the breach" to save Israel through prayer. To learn more about standing in the breach, study Psalm 106:21-23; Exodus 32:7-14; Ezekiel 13:3-6; 22:30-31. What is this mission? When and why is it necessary? Who was called to it in Israel? Does God call anyone to it now?

3. Study each of Ezra's and Nehemiah's prayers. Notice the purpose of each and the attitudes about self and God that each shows. Notice when, where, how, and why Nehemiah prayed. Compare the prayers of Abraham (see Genesis 18:20-33), Hannah (see 1 Samuel 1:11; 2:1-10), Hezekiah (see 2 Kings 19:15-19), David (in the Psalms), or Paul (in the New Testament Epistles).

4. List Ezra's and Nehemiah's character qualities and how each man exhibited those qualities. Then compare the qualities of other Bible leaders and teachers, such as Moses, Joshua, David, Jeremiah, Ezekiel, Peter, and Paul. You may want to focus especially on how all of them responded to adversity and compare that with the responses of Ezra and Nehemiah.

5. Nehemiah was a trusted official in the Persian court. To learn more about the life of a Jew in Persia, study Mordecai in the book of Esther. Or compare Daniel in the Babylonian court 150 years earlier (in the book of Daniel) or Joseph in Egypt 1,000 years earlier (in Genesis 39–50).

127

6. Study more closely the leadership of Ezra and Nehemiah in chapters 8–10 of Nehemiah to see how a revival of faith develops. Think about how a revival might occur in your church or community.

7. Study the major festivals commanded in the Old Testament. In what ways would these remind the Israelites about God and themselves? See Exodus 12:1-28; Leviticus 23:1-44; Numbers 28:16–29:40; Deuteronomy 16:1-17.

8. Study in their original context the laws about property and priorities that Nehemiah struggled to enforce. First think carefully about the Ten Commandments as presented in Exodus 20 and Deuteronomy 5. The other Old Testament laws were applications of these to Israelite culture. Think about the implications of putting nothing before God, of work and rest, of valuing life, of not coveting, and so on.

This might lead you to study the sabbatical and jubilee years in Leviticus 25. (Study Leviticus 19–27 for the context of how God wanted His people to order their society and what other values He wanted to instill.) Read in a Bible almanac or encyclopedia about life in Old Testament Israel to learn more of the context for these provisions. How can the principles then be applied in our culture today?

You might also look at the laws related to the lending of money in Deuteronomy 15:1-18 and 23:15–26:19. Or read Deuteronomy 4–11 for the context of how God and His people were related.

9. Study the concept of salvation in the Old Testament. Begin with the references in Nehemiah (see 1:9; 9:27-28); then move to Exodus, Deuteronomy, Isaiah, Jeremiah, and so forth. Look up in a concordance various forms of the words *save* and *deliver*. What did salvation and deliverance mean to the Old Testament people of God? What was their hope for salvation and deliverance?

10. Go back through the books of Ezra and Nehemiah and pick out key passages or verses to memorize. Some passages to consider: Ezra 3:10-11; 5:1-2; 6:14-16,19-22; 7:6,10,25,27-28; 8:21-23; 9:5-6,8-9; 9:13; 10:4; Nehemiah 1:4-11; 2:17-18; 4:4-5,15; 5:9; 6:3,9,16; 8:5-6,10; 9:5-6.

STUDY AIDS

For further information on the material in this study, consider the following sources. They can be purchased at such websites as www.christianbook.com and www.amazon.com, or your local Christian bookstore should be able to order any of them if it does not carry them. Most seminary libraries have them, as well as many university and public libraries. If a source is out of print, you might be able to find it online.

Commentaries on Ezra and Nehemiah

Joseph Blenkinsopp, *Ezra-Nehemiah: A Commentary* (The Old Testament Library, Westminster, 1988).

Mervin Breneman, *Ezra, Nehemiah, Esther* (New American Commentary, Holman, 1993).

David J. A. Clines, *Ezra, Nehemiah, Esther* (New Century Bible Commentary, Eerdmans, 1984).

F. Charles Fensham, *The Books of Ezra and Nehemiah* (New International Commentary on the Old Testament, Eerdmans, 1982).

C. F. Keil, *Ezra, Nehemiah, Esther* (Keil and Delitzsch Commentary on the Old Testament, Hendrickson, n.d.).

Derek Kidner, *Ezra and Nehemiah: An Introduction and Commentary* (Tyndale Old Testament Commentaries, InterVarsity, 1979).

J. G. McConville, *Ezra, Nehemiah, and Esther* (Daily Study Bible, Westminster, 1985).

H. G. M. Williamson, *Ezra, Nehemiah* (Word Biblical Commentary, Word Books, 1985).

Edwin M. Yamauchi, *Ezra-Nehemiah* (Expositors Bible Commentary, Zondervan, 1988).

Other Good Study Tools: A Sampling

I. Howard Marshall, A. R. Millard, J. I. Packer and D. J. Wiseman, eds., *The New Bible Dictionary* (InterVarsity, 1996).

Merrill F. Unger, R. K. Harrison, Howard F. Vos, and Cyril J. Barber, eds., *The New Unger's Bible Dictionary* (Moody, 2006).

Merrill C. Tenney and Moises Silva, eds., *Zondervan Encyclopedia of the Bible,* rev. ed. (Zondervan, 2009).

David and Pat Alexander, eds., *Zondervan Handbook to the Bible* (Zondervan, 2002).

John MacArthur, *MacArthur Bible Handbook* (Thomas Nelson, 2003).

George Knight and James Edwards, *Nelson's Compact Bible Handbook* (Thomas Nelson, 2004).

J. I. Packer, Merrill C. Tenney, and William White Jr., eds., *The Bible Almanac* (Thomas Nelson, 1980).

John D. Currid and David P. Barrett, eds., *The Crossway ESV Bible Atlas* (Crossway, 2010).

Historical Background Sources and Handbooks

Bible study becomes more meaningful when modern Western readers understand the times and places in which the biblical authors lived. *The IVP Bible Background Commentary: Old Testament,* by John H. Walton, Victor H. Matthews, and Mark Chavalas (InterVarsity, 2000), provides insight into the ancient Near Eastern world, its peoples, customs, and geography, to help contemporary readers better understand the context in which the Old Testament Scriptures were written.

A **handbook** of biblical customs can also be useful. Some good ones are the time-proven updated classic, *Halley's Bible Handbook with the New International Version,* by Henry H. Halley (Zondervan, 2007), and the inexpensive paperback *Manners and Customs in the Bible,* by Victor H. Matthews (Hendrickson, 1991).

Concordances, Dictionaries, and Encyclopedias

A **concordance** lists words of the Bible alphabetically along with each verse in which the word appears. It lets you do your own word studies. An *exhaustive* concordance lists every word used in a given translation, while an *abridged* or *complete* concordance omits either some words, some occurrences of the word, or both.

Two of the best exhaustive concordances are *Strong's Exhaustive Concordance* and *The Strongest NIV Exhaustive Concordance*. *Strong's* is available based on the King James Version of the Bible and the New American Standard Bible. *Strong's* has an index by which you can find out which Greek or Hebrew word is used in a given English verse. The NIV concordance does the same thing except it also includes an index for Aramaic words in the original texts from which the NIV was translated. However, neither concordance requires knowledge of the original languages. *Strong's* is available online at www.biblestudytools.com. Both are also available in hard copy.

A **Bible dictionary** or **Bible encyclopedia** alphabetically lists articles about people, places, doctrines, important words, customs, and geography of the Bible.

Holman Illustrated Bible Dictionary, by C. Brand, C. W. Draper, and A. England (B&H, 2003), offers more than seven hundred color photos, illustrations, and charts; sixty full-color maps; and up-to-date archaeological findings, along with exhaustive definitions of people, places, things, and events—dealing with every subject in the Bible. It uses a variety of Bible translations and is the only dictionary that includes the HCSB, NIV, KJV, RSV, NRSV, REB, NASB, ESV, and TEV.

The New Unger's Bible Dictionary, Revised and Expanded, by Merrill F. Unger (Moody, 2006), has been a best seller for almost fifty years. Its 6,700-plus entries reflect the most current scholarship and more than 1,200,000 words are supplemented with detailed essays, colorful photography and maps, and dozens of charts and illustrations to enhance your understanding of God's Word. Based on the New American Standard Version.

The Zondervan Encyclopedia of the Bible, edited by Moisés Silva and Merrill C. Tenney (Zondervan, 2008), is excellent and exhaustive. However, its five 1,000-page volumes are a financial investment, so all but very serious students may prefer to use it at a church, public, college, or seminary library.

Unlike a Bible dictionary in the above sense, *Vine's Complete Expository Dictionary of Old and New Testament Words,* by W. E. Vine, Merrill F. Unger, and William White Jr. (Thomas Nelson, 1996), alphabetically lists major words used in the King James Version and defines each Old Testament Hebrew or New Testament Greek word the KJV translates with that English word. *Vine's* lists verse references where that Hebrew or Greek word appears so that you can do your own cross-references and word studies without knowing the original languages.

The Brown-Driver-Briggs Hebrew and English Lexicon by Francis Brown, C. Briggs, and S. R. Driver (Hendrickson, 1996), is probably the most respected and comprehensive Bible lexicon for Old Testament studies. *BDB* gives not only dictionary definitions for each word but relates each word to its Old Testament usage and categorizes its nuances of meaning.

Bible Atlases and Map Books

A **Bible atlas** can be a great aid to understanding what is going on in a book of the Bible and how geography affected events. Here are a few good choices:

The Hammond Atlas of Bible Lands (Langenscheidt, 2007) packs a ton of resources into just sixty-four pages. Maps, of course, but also photographs, illustrations, and a comprehensive timeline. Includes an introduction to the unique geography of the Holy Land, including terrain, trade routes, vegetation, and climate information.

The New Moody Atlas of the Bible, by Barry J. Beitzel (Moody, 2009), is scholarly, very evangelical, and full of theological text, indexes, and references. Beitzel shows vividly how God prepared the land of Israel perfectly for the acts of salvation He was going to accomplish in it.

Then and Now Bible Maps Insert (Rose, 2008) is a nifty paperback that is sized just right to fit inside your Bible cover. Only forty-four pages long, it features clear plastic overlays of modern-day cities and countries so you can see what nation or city now occupies the Bible setting you are reading about. Every major city of the Bible is included.

For Small-Group Leaders

Discipleship Journal's Best Small-Group Ideas, Volumes 1 and 2 (NavPress, 2005). Each volume is packed with 101 of the best hands-on tips and group-building principles from *Discipleship Journal's* "Small Group Letter" and "DJ Plus" as well as articles from the magazine. They will help you inject new passion into the life of your small group.

Donahue, Bill. *Leading Life-Changing Small Groups* (Zondervan, 2002). This comprehensive resource is packed with information, practical tips, and insights that will teach you about small-group philosophy and structure, discipleship, conducting meetings, and more.

McBride, Neal F. *How to Build a Small-Groups Ministry* (NavPress, 1994). *How to Build a Small-Groups Ministry* is a time-proven, hands-on workbook for pastors and lay leaders that includes everything you need to know to develop a plan that fits your unique church. Through basic principles, case studies, and worksheets, McBride leads you through twelve logical steps for organizing and administering a small-groups ministry.

McBride, Neal F. *How to Lead Small Groups* (NavPress, 1990). This book covers leadership skills for all kinds of small groups: Bible study, fellowship, task, and support groups. Filled with step-by-step guidance and practical exercises to help you grasp the critical aspects of small-group leadership and dynamics.

Miller, Tara, and Jenn Peppers. *Finding the Flow: A Guide for Leading Small Groups and Gatherings* (IVP Connect, 2008). *Finding the Flow* offers a fresh take on leading small groups by seeking to develop the leader's small-group facilitation skills.

Bible Study Methods

Discipleship Journal's Best Bible Study Methods (NavPress, 2002). This is a collection of thirty-two creative ways to explore Scripture that will help you enjoy studying God's Word more.

Hendricks, Howard, and William Hendricks. *Living by the Book: The Art and Science of Reading the Bible* (Moody, 2007). *Living by the Book* offers a practical three-step process that will help you master simple yet effective inductive methods of observation, interpretation, and application that will make all the difference in your time with God's Word. A workbook by the same title is also available to go along with the book.

The Navigator Bible Studies Handbook (NavPress, 1994). This resource teaches the underlying principles for doing good inductive Bible study, including instructions on doing queston-and-answer studies, verse-analysis studies, chapter-analysis studies, and topical studies.

Warren, Rick. *Rick Warren's Bible Study Methods: Twelve Ways You Can Unlock God's Word* (HarperCollins, 2006). Rick Warren offers simple, step-by-step instructions, guiding you through twelve different approaches to studying the Bible for yourself with the goal of becoming more like Jesus.

Encounter God's Word
Experience LifeChange
LIFECHANGE by The Navigators

The LIFECHANGE Bible study series can help you grow in Christ-likeness through a life-changing encounter with God's Word. Discover what the Bible says, and develop the skills and desire to dig even deeper into God's Word. Each study includes study aids and discussion questions.

LIFECHANGE $9.99 OR $12.99

Genesis	9780891090694	1 Corinthians	9780891095590
Exodus	9780891092834	2 Corinthians	9780891099512
Deuteronomy	9781615216420	Galatians	9780891095620
Joshua	9780891091219	Ephesians	9780891090540
Ruth & Esther	9780891090748	Philippians	9780891090724
1 & 2 Samuel	9781615217342	Colossians & Philemon	9780891091196
1 & 2 Kings	9781615216413	1 Thessalonians	9780891099321
Ezra & Nehemiah	9781615217281	2 Thessalonians	9780891099925
Job	9781615216239	1 Timothy	9780891099536
Psalms	9781615211197	2 Timothy	9780891099956
Proverbs	9780891093480	Titus	9780891099116
Isaiah	9780891091110	Hebrews	9780891092728
Matthew	9780891099963	James	9780891091202
Mark	9780891099109	1 Peter	9780891090526
Luke	9780891099307	2 Peter & Jude	9780891099949
John	9780891092377	1, 2 & 3 John	9780891091141
Acts	9780891091127	Revelation	9780891092735
Romans	9780891090731		

Over 41 titles available. See a complete listing at NavPress.com.

Available wherever books are sold.

A NavPress resource published in alliance with Tyndale House Publishers, Inc.

Encounter God's Word
Experience LifeChange
LifeChange by The Navigators

Over 50 titles available. See a complete listing at NavPress.com.

Available wherever books are sold.   NAVPRESSⓄ

The Message Means Understanding

Bringing the Bible to all ages

*T*he *Message* is written in contemporary language that is much like talking with a good friend. When paired with your favorite Bible study, *The Message* will deliver a reading experience that is reliable, energetic, and amazingly fresh.

Available wherever books are sold.

NAVPRESS

NavPress - A Ministry of The Navigators

Wherever you are in your spiritual journey,
NavPress will help you grow.

𝒯he NavPress mission is to advance the calling of The Navigators by publishing life-transforming products that are biblically rooted, culturally relevant, and highly practical.

Available wherever books are sold. **NAVPRESS**

Available wherever books are sold.

NAV ESSENTIALS

Voices of The Navigators—Past, Present, and Future

NAVESSENTIALS offer core Navigator messages from such authors as Jim Downing, LeRoy Eims, Mike Treneer, and more — at an affordable price. This new series will deeply influence generations in the movement of discipleship. Learn from the old and new messages of The Navigators how powerful and transformational the life of a disciple truly is.

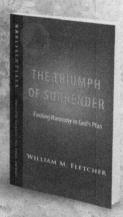

Meditation
by Jim Downing
9781615217250

Advancing the Gospel
by Mike Treneer
9781617471575

The Triumph of Surrender
by William M. Fletcher
9781615219070

Available wherever books are sold.   NAVPRESS

SUPPORT THE MINISTRY OF THE NAVIGATORS

The Navigators' calling is to advance the Gospel of Jesus and His Kingdom into the nations through spiritual generations of laborers living and discipling among the lost.

Navigators have invested their lives in people for more than 75 years, coming alongside them life-on-life to help them passionately know Christ and to make Him known.

The U.S. Navigators' ministry touches lives in varied settings, including college campuses, military bases, downtown offices, urban neighborhoods, prisons, and youth camps.

Dedicated to helping people navigate spiritually, The Navigators aim to make a permanent difference in the lives of people around the world. The Navigators help their communities of friends to follow Christ passionately and equip them effectively to go out and do the same.

To learn more about donating to The Navigators' ministry,
go to **www.navigators.org/us/support**
or call toll-free at **1-866-568-7827**.